ONE LAST GREAT THING

A Story of a Father and a Son,
a Story of a Life and a Legacy

JOHN BURKE

FREE PRESS

New York   London   Toronto   Sydney   New Delhi

Free Press
A Division of Simon & Schuster, Inc.
1230 Avenue of the Americas
New York, NY 10020

First Free Press hardcover edition November 2012

FREE PRESS and colophon are trademarks of Simon & Schuster, Inc.

For information about special discounts for bulk purchases,
please contact Simon & Schuster Special Sales at 1-866-506-1949
or business@simonandschuster.com.

The Simon & Schuster Speakers Bureau can bring authors to your live event.
For more information or to book an event contact the Simon & Schuster Speakers
Bureau at 1-866-248-3049 or visit our website at www.simonspeakers.com.

Photo credits appear on page 131.

Manufactured in the United States of America

1   3   5   7   9   10   8   6   4   2

Library of Congress Cataloging-in-Publication Data
Burke, John.
One last great thing: a story of a father and a son,
a story of a life and a legacy / John Burke.
p. cm.
1. Burke, Dick, 1934–2008. 2. Milwaukee (Wis.)—Biography.
3. Trek Bicycle Corporation. 4. Businesspeople—Wisconsin—Milwaukee—
Biography. 5. Philanthropists—Wisconsin—Milwaukee—Biography.
6. Heart surgery—Patients—Biography. 7. Fathers and sons. I. Title.
FS89. M653B87 2012
338.092—dc23
[B] 2012032993

ISBN 978-1-4767-1165-2
ISBN 978-1-4767-1164-5 (ebook)

This book is dedicated to:

My kids, Richie and Courtney.
May you remember the lessons of your grandfather.

Fran, The Big Guy's nurse
who took the best care of my dad

My wife, Tania, who is my best friend
and was my rock for those eighty-eight days

Dr. Lilly, who fought like a warrior
to save my dad's life

My mother, Lainey. I have learned as much
from my mother as from my father.

The Big Guy,
who taught me the lessons of life

I want to be remembered as someone who was fair and made a difference.

—Dick Burke, May 2000

Preface

My father died in March 2008 after an eighty-eight-day stay in the ICU of Froedtert Hospital in Milwaukee. My dad was a legend and his last eighty-eight days added to the story of an incredible life. His life was filled with so many great lessons that in the end I decided that I should write a book for my two children, Richie and Courtney. I wanted to make sure that they had a chance to learn as much from their grandfather's life as I have.

As I pounded out the book in my spare time over the past couple of years, it became clear to me that the story might be good enough that others might enjoy reading it. This book takes you through a great relationship between a father and a son. It takes you through the building of Trek Bicycle, and most importantly it tells the story of how my father and how our family dealt with his fight for life, and ultimately how my father and how our family dealt with his death. Death is a destination that we all share and yet there is little written about it and so many people are unprepared to deal with it. My father amazed me throughout his life, but he saved his best act for last. The way he dealt with his death is a story that should be of some help to any family facing this most difficult time.

Preface

Thomas Jefferson once said that the greatest skill a man can have is using one word instead of two. I try to write by that rule. This is a book that can be read in a night or over a weekend. It is a short read and right to the point. My father was that kind of a guy and so am I.

I am planning to contribute all the money I receive from the publication of this book to charity. One of my father's lessons was *to whom much is given, much is required.*

At his seventieth birthday party my father made two predictions: one was that he would do one last great thing. He wasn't sure what it was, but he had one in him. I believe that his last great thing was the way he died, and the lessons he left behind.

I hope that you enjoy the book.

JB

One Last Great Thing

Prologue

Bevil Hogg and Dick Nolan, Trek's first two employees.

When I was twelve years old my father came home from work one night and proclaimed that we were going to buy bicycles. He and I were going to go on a bicycle trip. "Okay, Dad," I told him. The only bike I had was my old red Schwinn single-speed with a silver banana seat and a slick tire in the rear. That bike was my transportation—to the football field, to friends, to the tennis courts, and to school. My red Schwinn was also my vehicle to the new and exciting world of danger. I grew up in the days of Evel Knievel, and as a big fan of TV's *Wide World of Sports* I would always tune in when Evel Knievel was on.

After the show, I would head out to our quiet road and set up a jump. There was a nice downhill on the road so I would place the jump at the bottom of the hill. I would always try and clear something, just as Evel Knievel did. Evel jumped trucks and canyons; I jumped garbage cans. I know I jumped two, but I don't know if I ever cleared or even attempted three. What I do know is that I never really crashed, which probably means that I never pushed the envelope too far.

As we drove down to pick out bicycles, my dad told me that he had met a guy named Bevil Hogg, a South African who owned a bicycle store in Madison, Wisconsin. Bevil was looking for someone to invest in his store. I had my mind on a new bicycle and didn't really pay any attention. We bought two bicycles that day. I remember that my dad bought a yellow Fuji, and while I cannot remember what I walked out with, I do know that it was an upgrade from the Schwinn. We bought some Eclipse bicycle packs and a few maps, and my dad announced that the following week we would be riding from Beaver Lake up to Fond du Lac and back. It is a beautiful ride through the hills and valleys of the Kettle Moraine region. I don't think that I had ever ridden my bike more than ten miles in one crack and now we were going to ride seventy miles in a single day. I don't remember much about this trip, with the exception that I crashed going over some railroad tracks, and that we were on a really busy road for the last few miles of Day 1 when a semi came past me and almost blew me off the road. On the second day of our two-day journey, we stopped at a bar outside of Monches. I drank root beer, and my dad had a couple of beers before we got back on the bikes and headed home.

We had a great time, my dad and I. He would always say that I was his best friend. He liked spending time with me, and I liked spending time with him. We played football in the drive, we played golf and tennis, we went to ball games, and lastly and most importantly, we played Ping-Pong. He loved Ping-Pong and we played thousands of games over the years listening to Arthur Fiedler and the Boston Pops or his favorite album of Irish songs. We *were* best friends.

Not long after the bike ride, my dad told me that he had bought a bike store in Madison with Bevil named Stella Bicycle Shop. My dad loved business and was always looking for great opportunities. After he graduated from college, he took a job with Caterpillar in Peoria, Illinois, where he was a credit manager. That only lasted a couple of years and soon he was in Madison working for Mautz Paint, again as a credit manager. In 1959 he left Mautz and returned to Milwaukee, where he had attended school at Marquette, to become the credit manager at Roth Distributing.

My dad had been at Roth for two months when Mr. Roth dropped dead of a heart attack. Red Schmalzer, the sales manager, asked my dad if he wanted to become partners. Did he have any money? My parents had saved up $10,000 over the previous few years by spending only the money my mom earned working full-time as a secretary, while putting my dad's paychecks in savings. My dad also asked both his parents and my mother's parents for a loan of $5,000 each. This was a big deal at the time, yet they both came through with the cash.

Life was good. Red was the ultimate salesman, and my dad was Mr. Operations. They ran a good business and it grew and grew. By the mid-1970s they had taken a small distributor located in Milwaukee and acquired operations in Minneapolis, St. Louis, and Denver. Yet my dad was always looking for more. When serendipity led to him meeting Bevil Hogg on a plane one day, my dad decided to pursue his interest in bicycles. After beginning with one store in Madison, they opened a second Stella Bicycle Shop in Champaign, Illinois. My dad always thought big, and his idea was to set up a nationwide chain of bicycle stores in college towns. One problem, though. It didn't work. The stores lost money and my dad and Bevil closed them in the fall of 1975. My father and Bevil learned that in order to succeed, they could not just sell any brand; they needed something special. None of the good brands were available to purchase, so Bevil's solution was to create their own brand of bicycles. No one was building really good bikes in the United States. Bevil thought that instead of being a retailer, they should manufacture high-end bikes built in the United States. Schwinn sold a lot of low-end bikes and kids' bikes and there were some high-end European brands, but nothing from the middle price points all the way to the top that was made in America. It was a unique idea, something completely different. The Big Guy had spent his life selling and distributing other people's products; now he was going to create and manufacture his own bicycle brand.

My father and Bevil found a big red barn in Waterloo—between Madison, where Bevil lived, and Hartland, where my dad lived—in which to start up the operations. The planning team was made up of my dad, Bevil, and Dick Nolan, who was the first factory manager. On a winter's night in 1975 my father and Bevil met at the Pine Knoll Supper Club, a few miles from Waterloo, to finalize the name. After drinking a couple of beers and reviewing a long list, they had two finalists—Trek and Kestrel. Bevil was from South Africa. Trek meant a long journey. Kestrel was a South African bird. Bevil liked Kestrel, the Big Guy liked Trek. Trek it was.

The first bikes were built in the red barn in Waterloo in 1976. The team decided to use silver-brazed lugged construction, which was similar to what many custom frame builders were using at the time. The bikes were hand painted with DuPont Imron paint and were absolutely beautiful. The first bikes were sold as kits—customers received a frame in one box and a parts kit in the other box. Retailers assembled the kits into a bike. The Big Guy and Bevil had succeeded in building a special brand. Beautiful hand-built bicycles, at affordable prices, built in the United States. No one was doing this and Trek was off to the races.

The first customer was Elmer Sorensen at Penn Cycle in Minneapolis. Elmer was an airplane mechanic for Northwest Airlines and was the salt of the earth. He started the bike business out of his garage as a hobby and grew Penn Cycle into one of the largest bicycle retailers in the country. Elmer became Trek's first customer with an order of six bicycles in the fall of 1976.

In the first year, Trek sold 904 bicycles. By 1979 Trek sales had taken off around the country. The idea of building high-quality bicycles in the United States appeared to be a good one, and the future looked bright. In 1979, with sales approaching ten thousand units, Trek moved out of the red barn and into a new factory on Madison Street. One day as we drove to the ballpark, my dad told me that his goal was to sell one hundred thousand bikes. Trek was on its way.

As Trek grew my dad also continued to grow his distribution business. But as usual, he was restless. His new project? Going back to school. While never a great student in college, The Big Guy had since turned into quite the learner. Newspapers, books, magazines—he could not stop reading and learning. The guy who barely graduated from Marquette was now going to the Sloan School of Management at MIT in Cambridge, Massachusetts. MIT proved to be a pivotal year for my dad. He met a number of people who would become key to his future. One was Doug Kinney, an investment banker who lived in Chicago. Doug would become a Trek board member and a key advisor over the years. It was also at MIT that my dad made one of his best business deals. One night while studying at the library, he was browsing through the Standard & Poor's books, which listed every company on the stock exchange. For fun he started at the beginning of the book looking at company profiles. When he got to the start of the Bs, Baker Brothers Distributing in Jacksonville, Florida, caught his eye. A heating and air-conditioning supplies distributor, it had a stock price that valued the company lower than its book value. My dad was always a value buyer and he thought it crazy that Baker Brothers, a simple distributor, was selling below book value. At the time, Roth was sitting on a good amount of cash, so my father had Roth start to purchase Baker Brothers stock. Less than two years later Roth ended up buying Baker Brothers. It turned out to be a great acquisition, a good company with some great people. The Big Guy helped to increase profitability, and the profits from Baker and from Roth would help to grow Trek.

I had gone to high school in Boston while my dad was at MIT, and I loved it. In 1980 I headed to Boston University. I sometimes get asked, Why BU? Simple. I applied to four schools and got into one. I had always liked bicycles, and at BU I became a member of the bike team. It was a club sport, and while I was not a super athlete, I ended up racing on the B team. I had a great time. The highlight of my career was a fourth-place finish at the West Point road race sophomore year.

During the summer of my junior year I worked at Trek in a new division called the Trek Components Group. This was a small subsidiary of Trek that supplied parts to bicycle retailers, and I worked in the warehouse. It was that summer that I fell in love with the bike business. My manager was Chuck, and the UPS guy's name was Frank. Every day when Frank would come by to pick up shipments, he and I would play a quick game of PIG on the basketball hoop. After finishing my day in the warehouse, I would head to the office to work the phones, calling retailers and trying to sell parts to whomever I could. It turned out that I was really good at it, and as a bonus at the end of the summer I was sent out to travel with legendary Trek salesman Harry Spehar.

Harry was great at selling bikes but not so good at selling

parts. I spent one week with Harry traveling in Northern California and I sold more than Harry did for the entire year. I had caught the bug. I returned to school for my senior year, and as a requirement of the business class I was taking, I needed to come up with an idea and write a business plan. I picked a bicycle accessories distributor and called it Quality Components (funny that twenty years later a bicycle parts distributor would become one of Trek's major competitors; its name is Quality Bicycle Products). There was a business competition called the Hinds Prize and you could enter the competition with your plan. If selected as a finalist you would present to the committee. Long story short, I ended up winning and collecting a check for $2,500. It was the end of my senior year, and I went out on top.

I had my heart set on working at Trek after graduation. But my dad had one simple rule: "Your last name gets you in the door; the rest is up to you." I graduated on a Sunday, was home in Wisconsin on Monday, had my wisdom teeth pulled on Tuesday, and started work on Thursday. My first full-time job at Trek was as a field sales rep for the Rocky Mountain region, which included Colorado, Utah, New Mexico, Wyoming, and parts of Idaho, Nebraska, and Texas. I was fired up and ready to sell. My training program at Trek consisted of two days in the office. I can clearly remember my first day. Bill Graham, the VP of sales, took me out to lunch with a group of people from the office. When the waitress asked me what I would have to drink at lunch I went with a beer. Big mistake. I was the only one who'd ordered a beer. It was the last beer I ever ordered for lunch.

Off to Colorado I went. I spent the first week traveling with my sales manager, Joel Holden, to visit customers. First I had to pick up the old Chevrolet Cavalier station wagon at the airport. I found the car, but it took me two hours to figure out how to put the car in reverse. Joel had two pieces of advice that have stayed with me to this day. First, tell your customers that you want to be the best rep that they have ever had. Then ask them for any advice. I did that and it worked like a charm. The second piece of advice is that the best sales reps drive on Sunday. I was too dumb to question my boss, so I drove on Sunday. Every other week to Utah, then to New Mexico. Each Sunday around noon, I would load up the Cavalier and drive. Always in my mind . . . "The best reps drive on Sunday."

Our main competitor at the time was Schwinn, and Schwinn retailers loved dealing with Schwinn. Quality was good, product was delivered on time, invoices were accurate; the list went on and on. The only problem with Schwinn is that consumers did not want to buy Schwinns at higher price points. They wanted to buy Treks.

I had joined Trek at the peak. Sales were around $20 million in 1984, and approximately fifty thousand Treks were being sold in the United States. Sales were up almost 30 percent from the year before and the company had big growth plans. But there was one small problem. Trek really didn't like the bicycle retailers that it was dealing with, and the retailers didn't like Trek. The service was poor, and there were problems with product quality. Trek had grown arrogant, and the problems were starting to show. It took forever for Trek to ship product. Sometimes I would write an order and show up at the customer two weeks later, but the order I had written on the last sales call still had not yet arrived. Product quality continued to get worse. Paint problems, frames out of alignment, credits that had been promised that never came through. I worked hard and sold a lot of product but the problems from the home office kept mounting. The more upset the retailers became, the harder Trek pushed. It was a recipe for disaster, and I had a front row seat. I watched the company that I worked for and the company my father founded fall from grace. Over the next year and a half I drove my Cavalier all over the Rocky Mountains watching Trek fall apart. In retrospect I could never have received a better education.

It was in January of 1985 that I received a promotion to move from Boulder to Waterloo and head up customer service. I was fired up. I had had my head handed to me for all of Trek's problems over the past year and a half, and now I could do something about it. I was ready to go back to Wisconsin and make a difference. I had one simple message to my customer service group: "Home of the happy customer." We were going to start taking care of the customer. Today. While it used to take up to a week to get an order shipped, we started shipping orders on the same day. If the warehouse was jammed, we left the office to work in the warehouse to make sure the orders went out on the same day. Credits that used to take up to a month to issue were now issued on the same day. If we were behind, people worked on Saturdays. We did whatever it took to take care of our customers.

While customer service was getting better, the financial

performance of the company was not. My dad had seen enough. I will always remember that I was out in California visiting customers in the Bay Area when the phone rang at the hotel. It was my dad. He never called me when I was on the road. "John, get on the first plane home tomorrow. I want to talk to you about some changes." I returned home and we met at the Nau-Ti-Gal restaurant outside of Madison. My dad told me that he was going to replace the management team and that he would be running the day-to-day business at Trek. He wanted me to run the sales and marketing organization. Could I do it, and who would I put in place? I was only twenty-four, but I was not short on confidence. Sure I could do it. Would love to. I gave him my plan. I would promote Giovanna D'Angelo, who was my best inside rep, to take my place as customer service manager. Gio was super smart, was great with people, and did whatever I asked her to do and more. She was a rock star. Pat Sullivan (Sully) would be my right-hand sales manager. Sully had worked at Trek for three years and was a sales guy. He loved to sell stuff and he loved to make people happy. He also worked like a dog and was the most loyal person you could ever have on your team. The third piece of the leadership team was Dick Moran. I had met Dick in kindergarten and we had been best friends ever since. Dick needed a job after college and The Big Guy found one for him at Trek. Dick turned out to be a sales machine selling parts and accessories. We expanded his duties, and the four of us—Gio, Sully, Dick, and I—would be the team on the field. "Great, you will take over on Monday," my dad replied. Sure enough he made all the changes, and there I was on Monday in charge of all the sales and marketing for Trek at the age of twenty-four.

A few days later, my dad gathered all the employees in the warehouse. There must have been 125 people. He stood up on a couple of crates and told them of all the company's problems, took responsibility for them, and said that he had three options. First, he could shut the company down; second, he could sell the company; or third, he could fix it. "I am not going to shut the company down, so cross that option off. I am not going to sell it because it is in such bad shape that no one will buy it, so take that option off the board. I am left with fixing the business, and here is how we are going to do it. We are going to make a quality product, at competitive values, deliver it on time, create a great atmosphere for our customers and our employees, and make a profit. Any questions?" There were none.

In a five-minute address my dad had apologized for the problems, taken responsibility, and laid out the strategy for turning the company around. It was vintage Dick Burke. Simple and to the point. Over the next five years every decision at Trek would follow his straightforward vision. Quality product, competitive value, on-time delivery, great atmosphere for the employees, and happy customers. Lousy product that had made it out the door was stopped, product that had been overpriced was discontinued, and new product was developed that hit the right price points. My dad was firmly in charge.

Things got so bad at Trek in 1985 and 1986 that we saw our retailer base drop from 900 to 450. In 1987 we stabilized the business and put all the chips on 1988. We introduced the Model 1200 aluminum road bike—black with magenta decals at $599. This model symbolized the turning point of the company. A real quality product competitively priced. My dad priced it at $599 even though the margin was really thin. We had planned to sell 3,000 units for the year, but by year's end we had sold over 12,000. We also had planned to build our retail group back up, and Sully and I had a vision of going from four hundred retailers up to one thousand in a single year. In a particularly memorable meeting with my dad, he asked about our dealer plan, and so I laid it out. It involved a great trade campaign based on the theme "Are you selling the bike more people want to buy?" and a really good dealer manual that explained all of the products and services that we were adding and improving.

We had initially planned to send our new material out to current and former Trek retailers. But Sully wanted to send it out to all the bicycle retailers across the United States. "Let's see who's interested, and if some Trek retailers get upset that we sent it to potential retailers in close proximity, then we will know that they really want the line." We had very little to lose and so we sent out over five thousand packets to retailers around the country. The next day as packets started to arrive in the Midwest, our phone lines lit up. The second day, more calls, the same with the third. We were buried with people interested in Trek. By the end of 1988, we had added over 650 retailers and had a total of 1,058 retailers in the US. Sully's target had been exceeded. We almost doubled the company's sales in one year. We went from $20 million to $38 million. Trek was clearly back in the game.

It was in the summer of 1988 that I was invited by Richard Schwinn to visit the Schwinn headquarters in Chicago to discuss the future of trade shows with industry leaders. I drove down to Chicago and was a little nervous when I arrived at the new Schwinn headquarters. Schwinn was the eight-hundred-pound gorilla in the US bike market. Sales there were three times that of anyone else, and they dominated the market. Before the meeting Richard gave the group a tour of the new offices. As the tour came to an end I said to Richard, "You have some really nice offices here." Richard replied, "We have to keep moving ahead after all; we have little guys like you nipping at our heels." To this day, I remember exactly what I said to myself: *someday I will bite that guy in the ass.*

In 1988 a small bike distributor from Switzerland, Paul Hubacher, sent me a fax. Would Trek be interested in selling bikes in Switzerland? Sure, we were opportunistic and Europe seemed as far away as the moon. The fax went back. "We would love to sell you some bikes. Here is a price list, let us know what you would like." Paul ordered sixty bikes for air shipment. About two weeks later, he ordered one hundred bikes for air shipment, then two weeks later another three hundred bikes air-shipped. By the end of the season Paul had ordered a lot of bikes. I may not be the brightest bulb in the box, but I figured if we were selling that many bikes in Switzerland, there must be a good bike market in the rest of Europe.

In September I headed off to Europe on my first overseas business trip. I spent time in the UK, where I met with a few potential Trek distributors, including Malcolm Davies, who sold me on the idea of opening a Trek office in the UK. From the UK, I went to Germany and toured bike shops. Sure enough, there was a market for Trek in Germany. The plan was simple: open the UK and Germany offices for the 1989 season. We took care of that, and they were a big success. We decided to keep on moving and so I hired my sister Mary, the brains of the family, to move to Europe and run the business. Mary and her team opened Austria, Spain, the Benelux, and France the following year. Trek's business in Europe took off.

With Europe on fire, I went to Japan to figure out what we should do there. It was at a time when American car companies were getting killed in Japan and everyone was screaming about what a difficult place Japan was to do business. I interviewed five different distributors and came to the conclusion that we should just open up our own business. I was concerned because everyone else had said not to go direct—it is too hard to do business in Japan. But we had no good options and I wanted to do business in Japan, so we decided to go direct and open our own business. The Japanese loved our product, especially road bikes. We sold a lot of expensive road bikes and expensive city bikes. We grew the business very quickly. Over the years, not only has it proved easy to do business in Japan, but Japan has been one of Trek's most profitable markets.

At the same time as we were opening new markets, we had a major product-development project in the works. A small team of people within Trek was working on a carbon-fiber bike. Carbon was complicated, but it held great promise as a material for bikes because it was super lightweight, it didn't wear out, and it provided a really smooth ride. The brains behind the new product were Jim Cole-grove and Bob Read. It had been a three-year project and by 1992 we were ready to show the world what the future of carbon-fiber bicycles would be. The new 5200 and 5500 were introduced as part of the 1992 model year and did extremely well. Trek was one of the very few companies manufacturing carbon-fiber bikes in the early nineties. All of our competitors said carbon was the wrong material. Too expensive and the bikes would break. By the end of the decade practically every high-end road bike made in the world was made of carbon fiber.

Trek grew like a weed in the early 1990s. Europe and Japan continued with strong growth. We proceeded to add new markets around the world. South America, Russia, South Africa, Australia, the list grew every year. By 1995 Trek was being sold in over eighty countries. The one product segment that grew the most in the early 1990s was the mountain-bike business. Invented by a small group of people in Marin County in the early 1980s, mountain bikes took off in the mid-eighties and the early nineties. One of the inventors of the mountain bike was Gary Fisher. Gary started his own brand of bikes in the early eighties and like most inventors Gary was great with product, but not so good on the business side. In 1994 we received a call about buying Fisher Mountain Bikes. I thought this was a pretty good idea. Trek had the reputation of being a Midwest company and mostly road bikes; Fisher was West Coast and all mountain bikes. Seemed like it might be a good fit. I talked to The Big Guy about it and he liked the idea. He had grown his distribution company by making acquisitions and no one liked a business deal more than The Big Guy. We met with Gary in Madison and quickly came to the conclusion that he was a good guy and that we could do business with him. The Big Guy hammered out an agreement in less than a day to buy the company. Over the next five years we built the Fisher brand from one of the smallest bike companies in the US to a top-ten brand. Great product, a really good image, and Trek's distribution made Fisher a success. Gary also was a big asset to the Fisher business. Gary worked hard marketing the brand and had lots of great product ideas that turned out to be winners.

We started thinking that it would be a good strategy to have multiple brands and so we kept looking for opportunities. Within two years we added Bontrager, a small builder of steel mountain bikes and components, and Klein, a high-end manufacturer of aluminum road and mountain bikes located in the state of Washington, and we signed a licensing deal with Greg LeMond to develop a line of road bikes. Trek business was seeing significant growth based on making acquisitions and a booming international business. As the business increased, a decision was made to ramp up production and add a new manufacturing plant in the town of Whitewater, which is about one hour down the road from Waterloo. The plan was high volume, lower cost production. This was a change from our current manufacturing strategy of focusing on low-volume, expensive bikes and having a manufacturing partner take care of our volume needs. Whitewater was a big plant, with state-of-the-art equipment and lots of capacity. The first new Treks rolled out of Whitewater in the summer of 1995.

The year 1995 turned out to be a historic year at Trek. Carbon road bikes started to catch on and we came out with a new blockbuster product. The Y Bike. The Y Bike was the first real carbon-fiber mountain bike and it had a super cool shape that looked like a Y. People loved the Y Bike. It was unique, it was beautiful, and it rode well. We started the year thinking we would sell 5,000 units and the actual sales exceeded 15,000 bikes. Trek was booming. The multi-brand strategy was working, our international business was growing, we had a lot of new products in the market, and the future never looked so bright. It was also Trek's most profitable year. The customers were happy, the employees were happy, The Big Guy was happy.

By 1996 Trek had grown to over $300 million in sales. A Japanese friend once told me that when it is sunny prepare for rain, and when it is rainy prepare for sun. By the end of 1996, it started to rain. After the great success of 1995 we ramped up our 1996 budgets by 20 percent. In order to hit those numbers, we would produce 20 percent more product and we would also spend more money on the sales and marketing side. As the year kicked off, we started to miss the sales forecast. We had never really missed sales projections in the past, and we were slow to react. Manufacturing continued to pump the bikes out and inventory levels went through the roof. By the end of the year, we had a mountain of inventory left, and in the bicycle business most of the product changes every year. We had to start discounting heavily to move the product. We had fewer sales than we had projected, and we had to lower prices in order to sell out of the 1996 product line. Profit margins plummeted because of the price reductions, and problems started to creep up everywhere. In retrospect Trek had gotten too big too fast. We made a major mistake by opening up Whitewater and trying to manufacture low–price point bikes, and we had added significant complexity to our business by making a large number of acquisitions. We got out of 1996 making a profit, but the future was no longer bright, and storm clouds were on the horizon. The current organizational structure at Trek was that The Big Guy was the chairman and Tom Albers was the president. Tom handled finance and manufacturing, and I took care of the rest. It was a clumsy reporting structure because I would still meet with The Big Guy once a week to give him the updates. It was at this time that my dad was looking to make a change and name me president of the company. And so in May 1997, I became president of Trek. It was my dream job. It was a job that I had wanted ever since I moved back to Waterloo, and now I had it.

Only one small problem. Trek was a mess, and it would get much worse before it got any better.

As predicted, 1997 was a disaster. At the end of every month I would meet with Joe Siefkes, our CFO, to go over the financial statements. Every month was twice as bad as we had projected. If we thought we would lose $300,000 in July, we lost $600K. When we put together a new forecast for the year and it predicted we would lose $5 million, we lost $10 million. It was not a pretty picture. Trek had never lost this kind of money and my father had been in business a long time and had never seen these kinds of losses. The stress level was high. I would still meet with

The Big Guy once a week and give him an update. We started to make a lot of changes throughout the company. We reduced production in Whitewater, we revamped our new product development process, we reduced lead times, and we cut expenses, but unfortunately it continued to get worse. We lost more money in 1998. After two years of heavy losses people were getting tired. The banks were not happy, the board was not very happy, and my dad wasn't real happy either. The weekly meetings to update him on progress were not a fun family event. The Big Guy was a numbers guy and no matter how much I would tell him about all the changes we were making for the future, he wanted to talk numbers. The numbers were always bad. I was doing my best, but that was not good enough. People wanted to see results. It was at the board meeting in July of 1999 that Doug Kinney, an outside director, said that if Trek did not make a profit in 2000 I would be fired. Someone needed to be responsible. I returned home and wrote a note to Doug and said that I agreed with him. If we did not make a profit in 2000, I would be done.

I had hired Tim Callahan in 1998 to take over manufacturing. Tim was an Irish guy from Massachusetts who had worked for GE for years and was a no-bullshit kind of guy who got stuff done. He knew manufacturing inside and out and he knew systems. Tim was the right guy at the right time. On Tim's first day at Trek, there was also a board meeting. My assistant Cindy walked in the room with a note from Tim. "There is a bomb threat at the Whitewater plant." I sarcastically scribbled back, "Move all the bad inventory into the plant ASAP." The bomb threat turned

out to be a dud. Tim did not; he was a rock star. Tim not only turned manufacturing around, he also brought in the concept of Kaizen, Japanese for "continuous improvement," which we used to turn the factories around. When it was clear that Kaizen was the winning formula for the factories, Tim told me, "You know the really great companies use Kaizen in the office to get rid of waste." Kaizen had made such a huge difference in the factories in such a short time that I gladly approved the Kaizen move into the office. It made the same difference in the office that it had made in the factories. In the gift-that-keeps-on-giving department, we took Kaizen to our dealer network and it has continued to make an amazing difference to this day. At the same time that we were using Kaizen to transform the company, we came out with some great new products on the road side and the mountain side. The year 1999 looked like it would be an improvement. Sure enough the financial results started to get better, dramatically better. When Joe and I thought we were going to lose $400K in a month, we would only lose $200K; when we thought we might break even, we made $300K. We were off to the races.

While things started to get better all around the company during 1999, there was something outside of our control that would add to our momentum. In 1997 we had signed a sponsorship deal with the US Postal Service to sponsor a bike team. They had a good group of riders led by Lance Armstrong, who had just come back to the sport after sitting out for two years battling cancer. US Postal would race at the 1999 Tour de France, the first time Trek had appeared in the race. Lance won the opening time trial

and kept on going. He sealed the deal with a big win in the mountains at Sestriere, a ski town in the Italian Alps. Lance went on to win the Tour de France and Trek showed up on the front of *Sports Illustrated* and *The New York Times,* as well as on the Letterman show. It was a time of great pride at the company and put an exclamation point on our comeback.

Trek continued to grow and had a run of great years. The year 2000 was really good, 2001 was better, and the streak continued. We had a great run all the way through 2006. In 2006, even though the company was doing very well, it became painfully obvious that we could be doing a better job on the product side. My dad was an accountant, and I was a sales guy, but I was smart enough to figure out that we needed to pick up the pace on the product side. I met with Joe Vadeboncoeur, who was in charge of global products, and asked him a simple question: if we wanted to have the best-in-class product in every category that we compete in, how many people would we have to add? "Hmmm, that is an interesting question," he replied. "Let me get back to you on that."

I have always been a big Apple fan. Bought my first Mac in the summer of 1984 and have supported the products ever since. With Apple's success, it seemed obvious to me that when you have the *best* products, they are easier to market, they are easier to sell, and they are easier to collect the cash for. Joe came back to me a couple of weeks later and laid out a plan with an organizational chart requiring fifty additional people—high-priced engineers and designers who would come at an average all-in cost of

$100,000—about $5 million total. I met with my dad to go over the plan, and he said yes in about three minutes. He could debate over the color of carpet in a new building for an hour, but a big decision with a good story—that took just three minutes.

We started to ramp up the product efforts in late 2006, and by the summer of 2007 we were ready to show the first new breakthrough products. The first was the all-new Madone, which was our high-end road bike line, and the second was the Fuel EX, our high-end mountain bike line.

One of my proudest days at Trek was in June 2007 when we introduced the new Madone and the new Fuel EX. The Milwaukee Art Museum was packed. Retailers and the global press were amazed by the new products. I remember finishing up the introduction and walking out into the museum where the products were on display. It was incredible. The energy in the room was off the charts, and it was clear that we had two home-run products on our hands. Our best-in-class product strategy was working. I was very happy and so was my dad. As we did at most of these events at some point in the evening, we found ourselves—just me and my dad—standing in a corner with beers in our hands. He was, in his own words, "a happy camper."

The heart of my story begins here.

CHAPTER 1

The Seventieth Birthday

*The family at Riverbend for The Big Guy's
seventieth birthday.*

I called him The Big Guy. He was only five foot eight, but he liked the name and it fit him well. Short in size, big in personality. He was many things to many people. To me, he was always The Big Guy. At the time he was appointed the chairman at Quad/Graphics, a printing company in Milwaukee, he also had the same title at Trek, so I figured it was time to upgrade his nickname. And so one day around that time I began calling him The Chairman. As we finished a meeting one day, he called me over to the corner of the room and said to me, "You know that nickname The Big Guy? I really like it."

The Big Guy liked birthdays and he liked milestones. He had been looking forward to celebrating his seventieth birthday for quite some time. He had made a decision that the birthday would be a weekend event. The family was summoned, all of his kids and their spouses. There are five of us Burke kids—me and my four sisters. Kathy, the oldest and most social; Mary, the brains of the family who graduated near the top of her class at Georgetown and went on to Harvard Business School; Sharon, the free spirit of the family, or as The Big Guy would refer to her, the number-three daughter; and finally, Michele, the most caring, who lives next door to my mother. In addition there are nine grandkids. He had done so much for all of us that we decided to get him something special for the Big 7–0. We went back and forth until we decided to all chip in and get him a Mercedes convertible. Why a Mercedes convertible? His first great car in 1972 was a Mercedes SL 350. He loved that car, and he loved to drive it: to work, to tennis, to the Kiltie on many summer nights for ice cream, to school, as many as he could pack in—always in the Mercedes.

Now before my dad became The Big Guy, my nickname for him was Mr. Goodwrench. There was a commercial back in the day featuring Mr. Goodwrench, who would answer your technical questions. My dad was the opposite of Mr. Goodwrench: he could not fix anything! One beautiful autumn day in Boston, Mr. Goodwrench and I were returning home from a game of tennis. As we made our way into the drive, smoke came up from the hood of his beloved Mercedes. As we got out of the car, I could see flames coming out of the hood. My dad could not fix anything; nobody in the family could. So I dashed toward the garage and filled a garbage can full of water while my dad called the fire department. As I prepared to throw the water on the car Mr. Goodwrench stopped me and said, "Don't throw the water on the car. It might blow up." And so Mr. Goodwrench and I stood watching his prized possession go up in flames waiting for the Belmont fire department to arrive. When they did arrive the Mercedes was toast. He spent the next year trying to get it refurbished but it never worked out. The legend was lost.

As we gathered for his seventieth birthday dinner that evening, we sat around during cocktail hour and told stories of all of his cars. The Thunderbird that he had totaled twice; the Mercedes that burnt to the ground; the BMW that had its windows smashed at the airport and had its stereo stolen even though the door was unlocked and the keys were left in the ignition; the Jaguar that he drove to 170,000 miles; the Blazer that he never liked but drove to 140,000 miles; and the current green Mercedes SUV that he had driven to over 100,000 miles but of which he had recently left the sunroof open while taking it through a car wash. We laughed about each of the cars and all of the stories that went with them. It was the perfect setup for his gift. We then led him outside the restaurant, where we had a brand-new Mercedes convertible waiting for him with a big bow. It was over the top, perhaps a little too much, but for a man who had a lot of money and never spent it, he loved the gift. He had done so much for all of us and it was nice to give a little something back. To the kids it was a car, a wonderful birthday gift for number 70. To The Big Guy it was much more. It was a symbol that his kids really did love him.

After a few laps around the parking lot we headed in for dinner. He took me aside and said to me, "This evening I would like to make a number of remarks." I said, "Okay, Dad," and did not think much of it. A little while later when he and I were away from the table he said the same thing: "This evening I would like to make a number of remarks." "Fine," I said, thinking to myself, *This is your birthday party and you can say whatever you want and whenever you want to say something.* So I suggested, "How about right after dinner and before dessert?" He liked that, a firm plan.

As dinner came to an end and the plates were cleared my father stood up from the table, and I will never forget this as long as I live. He put his right hand in his sport jacket and pulled out one of his famous yellow legal pages. My dad used yellow legal pads for forty years. He took copious notes, sent out thousands of memos—always on yellow legal pads. As the yellow pages came out of his jacket I noticed that the speech was more than one page. My first reaction was *You have got to be kidding me.* Here we are at a birthday dinner and he is going to give a talk like it's a sales meeting? What followed was amazing.

In front of his wife, his kids, and their spouses he took the group through his entire life. He went through the highs and the lows, from growing up in Chicago to working the summers in a grain elevator, from going to college to dropping out after a week and coming home. His mother took him to the priest to ask what to do with him and the next day he was enrolled at Marquette University in Milwaukee. He graduated with a low C average, and the best thing he did there was meet my mother. They got married and moved to Peoria, where he worked in the credit department for Caterpillar. From there, on to Madison, where he worked in credit at Mautz Paint. Next stop, Milwaukee, where he got a job at a small appliance distributor, Roth Distributing. It was at Roth that he caught his big break. He and Red Schmalzer grew Roth from a tiny appliance distributor with one location to one of the largest in the country. The Big Guy talked about starting Trek and the pride that he had in the bicycle business. He talked about divorcing my mother in front of his new wife. Vintage Big Guy. Brutally honest. Mostly, he talked about each of his kids and the pride that he had in the family that he had built.

The Big Guy went on to talk about giving back and all of his philanthropic efforts. He had a bunch. His goal in life was to give away all of his money. The way he did it was very low-key. He avoided the limelight. As his twenty minutes of remarks came to a close (how many people do you know who give a twenty-minute talk at their birthday party?) he said that he would make two predictions. The first was that he planned to live to 2020, which would make him eighty-six; the second prediction was classic Big Guy: "I will do one last great thing. I do not know what it is, but I have one left in me."

The end. Wow. It was an amazing speech. I knew how

good it was because the next day as I flew to Europe, I wrote down everything he said that I could remember. We finished the dinner with dessert and then he told me that this was the perfect evening. The only thing that would have made it better was Ping-Pong. My dad said, "For my seventy-fifth can we play Ping-Pong?" "Sure," I said, "we will have Ping-Pong for the seventy-fifth." As we walked down the stairs to the bar for an after-dinner beer there it was—a Ping-Pong table that we had brought in. It was the perfect night.

CHAPTER 2

San Francisco

*Dick Burke playing golf along the sea
in Monterey, California.*

Every year we head west for a Trek board meeting in
Monterey and 2007 was no different. This year my dad
was going to meet with a philanthropic group in San Francisco before the board meeting. I told him that I was going
to be with Tania (my wife) and my friend David and why
not pick him up in the city and take him down? We agreed
to have dinner the night before and drive to Monterey the
next day. It was a Monday night when we met him for
dinner. The Packers were playing the Broncos on *Monday
Night Football,* and we decided to have a few beers and

watch the game. Before we went out, he wanted to go for a walk with me. As we walked he said, "I have been having some breathing problems. When I run, I can't go very far before I feel short of breath. I went to the hospital and they took me through a number of tests and it appears that I have a problem with one of my valves. I have looked at all of my options and I have made a decision to get the valve replaced. This is the option that will give me the best chance at continuing my active lifestyle."

Being active was important to The Big Guy. Up until the early 1970s, he had been a pipe-smoking, beer-drinking, thirty-pounds-overweight kind of guy. That all changed when Frank Shorter won the Olympic marathon in Munich in 1972 and a running boom began in America. The Big Guy was on the front edge. He started by running out to the end of our road and back, 1.2 miles, and then graduated to running around Beaver Lake, exactly five miles. He became somewhat of a running legend in the area because no one else ran. His passion for running grew and he began to run distance races. I was there for his first big race—the Mayfair Half Marathon in Milwaukee. I followed him on my bike. This was long before Power-Bars and he gave me M&M's to carry for him in case he got hungry. He did well in that race and he set his sights on running a marathon. He always dreamed of running in New York, and in 1979 he ran his first of five New York City Marathons. He followed that up by running Boston three times in the 1990s.

Not being able to exercise was not an option for my dad. Dr. Youker, his good friend, had reviewed his case and had told him that he should consider the option of stents and get a second opinion. The Big Guy was never big on second opinions and he was confident that he was getting excellent medical advice, and that was the decision that he made. Vintage Big Guy. Make up your mind and stick with it. "It's not that risky but there is a one in one hundred chance that I will not make it." As the walk came to an end he said, "You are in charge of my medical decisions—remember the run?" Yes, I replied. We had gone running way back in the day when we were training for our first Boston Marathon. I remember it clear as day, when he stopped on Gorham Street in Madison and told me, *You are in charge of my medical decisions. If anything happens to me you make the calls. I don't want you to do anything just to keep me alive. I always want to lead an active life. That is important to me. If I can't lead an active life, pull the plug.* Okay, Big Guy. He liked to talk about death with me and I never really paid any attention to him. My dad was fit as a fiddle and ate extremely well. As we walked the streets of San Francisco that night, he was seventy-three years old and at the peak of his life. Trek was doing well, he was traveling all over the world, he had a great relationship with his kids, a great marriage with his new wife, Camille, and he was trying as hard as he could to give his money away.

We finished the walk and met Tania and David at the bar and watched the Packer–Bronco game on TV. We had a great time. The game went into overtime, and I went to the bathroom. I came back and on the first play, Brett Favre had thrown an eighty-two-yard touchdown pass to win the game. All in the span of time that I was in the bathroom.

Everyone got a big laugh out of that, and then we retired for the evening.

The next morning we got in the car and headed down to Monterey. My father was a very humble man. I believe it was Benjamin Franklin who once said that you judge the intelligence of a man not by what he says, but by the questions he asks. Ben Franklin would have loved my dad; he was the world's best listener and he loved to ask questions. However, on this morning, it was David who asked the question "Dick, how did you get your start in business?" "Well . . . ," he started, "I was a credit manager at Caterpillar in Peoria and then I moved to Madison and was the credit manager at Mautz Paint. That didn't last too long though. I think I quit before I got fired." He went on to tell David his entire business story. He talked for over an hour.

We arrived in Monterey and it was a beautiful day. We had a spectacular lunch at Pebble Beach and then played golf at Cypress Point. The Big Guy was a lousy golfer. He could have been good but he just didn't put in the time. He had other things to do. Although a lousy golfer, he was not a quiet golfer. He spent a lot of time talking to himself as he walked the course. Among his favorites: "Goddamn it, Dick!!!" and "Put the ball in the hole, you idiot!" And whenever he played at Cypress he would always bark at the seals as we walked the ocean holes. How many people do you know who bark at the seals while playing golf? The Big Guy was one of a kind. On that sunny day in Monterey my dad was happy, he was proud, he was at the top of his game.

CHAPTER 3

The First Surgery

My dad's first heart surgery was scheduled for November 14, early in the morning. I had been out of the country on business, and I returned late the night before. I had talked to him earlier in the week and he told me that it was no big deal—I did not need to be there. As I flew back from Europe I thought I really did want to see him before he went under the knife. He had told me that he needed to be there at 4:30 a.m. to check in for a 6 a.m. surgery. So I woke up that morning at 3:30 a.m. and made the drive from Madison to Milwaukee. When I walked into the room there he was joking with the nurse. I could see in his eyes that he was happy to see me. He would never admit it, but he was. We had a great time, laughing with the doctors and the nurses. I remember that a nun came by and he had a nice chat with her. He was all smiles, trying to keep loose, but I knew that underneath he was nervous. When they came to take him away he gave me a smile and his patented thumbs-up, and then The Big Guy was off.

The surgery lasted for six hours and was hailed as a complete success. I went by to see him the next day and he was tired and a little cranky but that was it. He was fine. I stopped by to see him again the day after that and he was better. He loved "good-looking blondes," and he had a few taking care of him. He ended up staying in the hospital for three days and then he was sent home.

At home he rested and became restless. My dad always needed to have something going on and he needed to be moving. I decided to send some people down from Trek to discuss certain issues with him so that he would have something to do. Joe Siefkes, the VP of finance, and Bob Burns, the general counsel, visited him a few times. Camille had some of his friends from philanthropic ventures stop by, and Joe Tierney, his lawyer, also visited. It was mid-November and it was getting cold. About a week after he had been discharged, I visited him at his house. He was up and walking, and he and I took a walk outside. He insisted that we walk to the end of the street. He was very slow, but we had a good time. As usual, we talked business, sports, and Trek. He was on track. He was supposed to leave for Florida before Christmas and he looked forward to recovering there. His recovery continued to go well.

CHAPTER 4

Hanging by a Thread

In early December I went to Europe for a series of meetings. Early in the week I called from Europe to say hello, and I talked to Camille. She told me that my dad wasn't feeling that well, but I didn't give it that much thought. I returned from Europe on Friday and planned to visit him on Sunday. Friday night at home I got a call from The Big Guy. "The nurse came by today and heard something in my heart that she did not like. The hospital just called and they wanted me to come in right away. Anyways, I am here at the hospital and they want to operate on me tomorrow just to make sure everything is okay. They think it should only take about an hour. They are going to start at eleven a.m. Don't worry about it though, it's not a big deal."

I told him that Courtney (my daughter) had a basketball game at 8 a.m. and then I would drive down to see him before the surgery. Once again he told me that I didn't need to come down, that it wasn't that big of a deal. Courtney's game ended at 9 a.m. and I got in the car and drove down to Froedtert Hospital in Milwaukee. I figured I would get there a little bit after ten and I would see The Big Guy before the surgery. As I was driving my cell phone buzzed—it was Camille. "They moved the surgery up, he is going into surgery in thirty minutes." I drove faster. I wanted to see him. I knew it meant a lot to him that I had showed up for the previous surgery, and I wanted to be there for this one.

I missed him by ten minutes. They had taken him away by the time I arrived. By this time most of the family was also there. Camille was there, Mary and Michele were there, and they said he seemed a little bit anxious but as always, he told everyone not to worry, it was not a big deal.

The Big Guy is a numbers guy. So am I. I time everything: how long it takes to go from point A to point B in a car, how long someone's speech is, how long it takes the restaurant to get me my first cold beer, the list goes on. While we all waited in the cafeteria, I kept my eyes on the clock. The surgery should have started at 11 a.m. and should have been done at 12:30. Twelve-thirty came and it went. No word from anyone. As the clock moved closer to one, Camille went to check with the family center. Again, no word. We waited and waited and the minutes seemed to move slower and slower. No word. At 2 p.m., three hours into the surgery, word came that the surgery was more complicated and that the valve had been infected. It was going to take two more hours and they should be done by five o'clock.

The concern level hit the roof. For the first time in my life I thought The Big Guy was in trouble. He always liked to talk to me about Trek stock and what would happen to it when he died. I was never really interested in this topic and I listened with little enthusiasm as he would go through his estate planning. I thought The Big Guy was like Rose Kennedy. I thought he would outlive us all. He was seventy-three, was in great shape, had great health habits, and was sharp as a tack. As I sat in the cafeteria, for the first time in my life I thought that maybe he might die.

The cafeteria became very quiet as the family focused on five o'clock. Five o'clock came and five o'clock went. Six o'clock came and six o'clock went. Still no word. At some point after six, close to seven hours into the surgery, word came again that "the surgery was more complicated than initially thought." The Big Guy's valve was being replaced. The surgery would continue and they did not know when it would end. Eight o'clock, nine o'clock, ten o'clock, eleven o'clock. He had now been in surgery for twelve hours. Word came through that they were just finishing up and he should be done sometime just after midnight. Midnight came and it went. One o'clock came and word came through that The Big Guy was finished with surgery. The doctor would be meeting with us once he was done.

We waited for a while in the family center, and in walked Dr. Lilly, who had just worked on my father for fourteen hours. He explained the situation. "I opened him up and his new valve was hanging by a thread. The area around the valve was completely infected. I am guessing that the valve was infected when it was put in." The original surgery had been complicated, but the success rate was 99 percent. It looked like The Big Guy represented the 1 percent. Dr. Lilly went on to say that it was too early to tell how The Big Guy was going to do. He was in danger and he might not survive. He had also spent twelve hours hooked up to a pump. Dr. Lilly explained that the longer someone is hooked up to the pump the worse off he is. "If he makes it, there could be brain damage, there could be kidney damage. It is too early to tell. We should know a lot more in the next forty-eight hours."

CHAPTER 5

The Long Drive Home

At two in the morning Tania and I left Froedtert Hospital and headed into Milwaukee to spend the night with Camille. As I drove toward his house I started to think about all the things that we had done together. The Big Guy always called me his best friend. When I was growing up we did just about everything together. We played tennis and golf. We played football on the road in front of the house. As I drove I started to think about Ping-Pong. Every night, and I mean every night, we played Ping-Pong. I would ask what music he would like to listen to and it would either be Arthur Fiedler and the Boston Pops Fourth of July Concert, John Denver, or a collection of Irish music. I am guessing that we played for ten years and the music selection never changed.

For the evening match it was a best-of-three series. When I was growing up if we played ten games, I would win eight. If I won the first two games there would always be a third game, and if I won the third game there would always be a fourth. The Big Guy was quite passionate about his game. His passion showed in the condition of the table. When he hit a bad shot on a big point he had the habit of slamming his paddle into the table. On more than one

41

occasion the paddle would take out a chunk of the table. After a few years we moved the table around so that he had a fresh side with no chunks. That would last a few years and then we would move the table around again until that side was chewed up. Our Ping-Pong table sat on top of a pool table, so it was two pieces with four sides. Over the years, my father chewed up all four sides. Visitors to the house would always start the game off with "What happened to your table?"

As the years passed, his love for the game did not. Every time he bought a new house he would have a Ping-Pong room. He had just purchased a new house in Milwaukee three months before he went into the hospital. It was being renovated and he had taken me over for the grand tour. As we toured the house he told me, "This will be my last house and I want to do it right." He showed me all of the rooms with great enthusiasm. And then . . . we reached the top floor, where he explained to me how the Ping-Pong table would be set up. The last time we played Ping-Pong was in Florida, where he had his table outside. At seventy-three years old, and even after a few beers, he cleaned my clock. Two games in a row. We played the third and then the fourth. Big Guy 4, JB 0. He would have played all night. I had had enough.

Tania and I continued on the drive home from the hospital and passed Marquette University. My dad was a Marquette graduate and we would always go to the basketball games. Milwaukee was cold in the winter, but The Big Guy would not pay for parking, so we would park as close to the arena as possible as long as the parking was free. Which meant that we would usually park a mile away and then make the long, cold walk past the Ambrosia chocolate factory. That was the one and only highlight of that walk. I loved those games. In those days Marquette basketball was the best. Al McGuire always had a great team and I lived and died Marquette basketball.

When I finally pulled into his driveway all I wanted to do was go to sleep. It had been a long day. I talked to Camille and we agreed to get up early and head back to the hospital to get the update.

CHAPTER 6

The Question

Lainey in Paris at the Tour de France.

The next morning we set up camp in the cafeteria and waited for word from my dad's doctors. Finally Dr. Lilly arrived to meet with the family. He let everyone know that The Big Guy was on the edge and it could go either way. He could die, yet even if he lived there might be brain damage or problems with his kidneys. The message was very clear. He would know more in a few hours. The doctor also announced that the family could visit my dad.

We got off the elevator and entered the ICU. The door swung open and we headed down the hall to Room 10, where The Big Guy was. I prepared myself for the worst, and that is just about what it was. He was hooked up to every machine that you could imagine. Tubes going in and out of him, a ventilator assisting with his breathing. He was being kept alive by life support. I had hoped that Dr. Lilly was making the situation out to be worse than it actually was, but he was not. I left the room and I cried my eyes out. I was not sure if he was going to make it. The family retreated downstairs to the cafeteria and waited for more information. We needed something to keep us busy and Mary or Kathy had brought Yahtzee. This was a game that we always played as kids, and now as our father lay upstairs fighting for his life, we sat in the basement cafeteria playing Yahtzee.

As I walked around the cafeteria wondering if The Big Guy would live or die, Camille came up to me and asked me a very simple question. "Would it be a good idea if your mother was here?" What a question!!!

My parents divorced more than twenty years ago. I still remember the day I received a phone call from my father with the news—I was sitting on my couch in Boulder watching a football game. I couldn't believe it, never saw it coming. My mother, Lainey, is the nicest person in the world. Even though The Big Guy could be a pain in the ass sometimes, they were my mother and father and it always seemed to me like they got along. After the divorce, they got along fine. At one point in time they even got back together and were "dating."

The Big Guy had met Camille eight years ago on a bike ride and they were married a couple of years later. Camille was always nice to me, but in retrospect I never gave her the respect that she gave to me. Inside, I guess I always had the feeling that she was not part of the family. Now at a time of our family's greatest crisis, the person who did more to bring the family together with one single sentence was Camille. I thought about this for at least three seconds and said, "Yes, that would be a very good thing." I called my mother and relayed the conversation that I had had with Camille, telling her to drive to the hospital right away. As my mother arrived in the cafeteria, she came in and gave Camille a big hug. It was a defining moment. It let everyone in the room know that what mattered most of all was The Big Guy. Camille brought the family together and set the tone for our journey. It was a gesture that I will never forget.

That Sunday morning my dad's brother Mike arrived. I had not seen Mike in a long time. He and The Big Guy were never that close, but over the past few years they had been getting together on occasion. I had always liked Mike. He taught me how to use a stick shift and he was always fun when he was around. On this very cold December day, we headed out to an Irish tavern for lunch. With the entire family assembled we sat around on a Sunday afternoon and drank beer and watched our beloved Packers get crushed by the Bears.

But what did we really do? We sat and wondered whether The Big Guy would live or die. As we left the hospital that day he was still alive, still fighting for his life. I knew that he would make it. I had seen my dad in crisis on many different occasions and he had always prevailed. Always. Before we left the hospital that night, we put together a schedule for the next couple of days to make sure that someone was with him at all times.

CHAPTER 7

On a Scale of One to Ten

Over the next couple of days The Big Guy made some progress. His doctor's biggest fear was that my father might have brain damage because of the twelve hours that he had spent on the mechanical pump that kept his heart going while his valve was being replaced. It became clear, though, that his head was fine. The game was going to come down to how his kidneys had survived, how his liver was, and whether or not he could fight off infections. On the Monday after the surgery, we were allowed to set up camp in The Big Guy's room in the ICU. My sisters did a great job of decorating. Pictures were brought in to fill the walls with memories of a great life. An iPod was installed to bring the room to life. Michele and her husband, Derek, put together a playlist with all of his favorites: John Denver, Barbra Streisand, Johnny Cash, some Irish music, Arthur Fiedler and the Boston Pops. The Big Guy's favorite stuffed animal, Fred the Bear, was brought in to stand guard 24–7. The command center had moved from the cafeteria up to the ICU.

For the next week, we kept vigil in the room waiting for some real progress. The big issue became his white-blood-cell count. He had developed an infection, and the number of white blood cells in his body increased or decreased in direct proportion to how bad the infection was. High white-blood-cell count bad, low white-blood-cell count good. It started at 25,000 and it would get better some days and worse on others. As the days passed we got closer to Christmas.

The talk among the group was whether or not Christmas should be scaled back or canceled. At Trek I use what we refer to as the Eisenhower rule, "What is in the best interest of Trek?" to make decisions. During our days at the hospital, the "What would The Big Guy want?" rule was put into place. Simple answer . . . he would have Christmas. And so on Christmas Eve after the entire family first visited the hospital to wish The Big Guy a Merry Christmas, we headed out to the family house.

Christmas Eve was always the favorite family holiday. The entire family—kids, grandkids, and always a few friends without a family—would gather at six for cocktails and appetizers. Each family would bring their contribution for the food and I would bring the beer. After dinner, we would gather in the family room with presents surrounding the tree and a bounty of cookies. Before the presents would be opened, Lainey would have me read *The Night Before Christmas* with the young kids helping me out. And then to the main event . . . the gifts. There was a rule in the Burke household about Christmas gift giving. You would draw a name at Thanksgiving and no gifts over $100. Some people abided by the rules . . . and some did not!

In comparison to other Christmas Eves it was a somber event, but in a weird way it was very special. For a family that had avoided crisis for the most part, and had been blessed in so many different ways, it was less about gifts and more about being thankful for what we had. Most importantly, Christmas Eve was all about thinking of The Big Guy, and in a way, thinking about my mother. Even though she was the picture of health, she was in her early seventies and I began to realize that she was not going to last forever.

After Christmas was over, one day started to blend into the next. The Big Guy's white-blood-cell count went up and his white-blood-cell count went down. No breakthroughs. Not much of a change. The Big Guy continued to be in a coma, hooked up to every machine you could imagine. They were trying just about everything. Doctors, nurses, infectious-disease specialists, physical therapists—the list went on and on. There were nurses at his side twenty-four hours a day. He had a great crew of nurses led by a woman named Fran. As my dad would say, it looked like Fran had the map of Ireland on her face. Short, a little stocky, big smile, and a bigger personality, Fran watched over The Big Guy like no one else could have. She was fun, optimistic, and tough. There were very few people in his lifetime who ever told The Big Guy what to do. Fran was one of them and he respected her for it.

As the days passed, we prepared ourselves for a very long battle. Dr. Lilly was very clear that this would take time and that there would be battles won and battles lost along the way. The goal was to win the war. In a meeting just before New Year's, with the family packed into the small third-floor conference room, I asked the question: what are his chances of living? My dad was a one-to-ten guy; everything in the world could be boiled down to a one-to-ten question. "How is your day going on a scale of one to ten? What would you give that restaurant on a scale of one to ten? On a scale of one to ten what do you think the chances are that the Packers will win on Sunday? On a scale of one to ten what is your confidence level that we will hit the sales number for the month?" On this day I asked Dr. Lilly, "On a scale of one to ten what are my father's chances of living?" Answer: "Four to five." I did not know how to interpret that. I hoped that Dr. Lilly was one of those under-promise over-deliver kind of people, and that his four to five meant more like a six to seven. I hoped.

CHAPTER 8

Breakthrough?

As we approached New Year's Day my sister Mary came up with the idea of buying a bottle of champagne for each of the staff who had worked on The Big Guy. It was over thirty bottles, and the staff loved it. As we passed the New Year not much changed. There were good days and bad days, but it was all basically the same—he was still in a coma and there was no movement. It was a Sunday morning in January when the phone rang. It was my sister Michele. "You need to come down here. Dad has woken up and he is writing some cryptic words on a piece of paper!" What did he write? "JB and lawyers." The drive from Madison to the hospital in Milwaukee was one hour and four minutes. I know because I had now done the round trip perhaps thirty times. I grabbed Tania and off we went.

This was it, the big breakthrough that we had been waiting for. When we got to the hospital there he was, sitting up with his eyes wide open. Wide open. The Big Guy was very tired, but he wanted to know what had happened to him. I did my best to let him know. He was so exhausted that he could not write anymore, and I did not want to push him. We were just so happy that he was back.

Over the next few days he was more alert. Sometimes he

would try to write, but that was so difficult that the hospital staff gave him a board and he would point to the letters. I can't say that they were great conversations, but he was back. I was sure that this was the first step on the way to recovery.

The days of writing short words and pointing at letters continued for about a week. The steady progress that we had all hoped for stalled and then he started to get worse. His white-blood-cell count went up and he was no longer able to communicate. We were moving in the wrong direction. While The Big Guy's health went up and down like a roller coaster, the family did not. Mary kept the schedule and the family was by his side from six in the morning until nine at night. As we headed into February, the days started to pile up. We had now been at this for over sixty days and he was not getting better. He developed problems with his kidneys, and he had to be hooked up to a dialysis machine all the time. His lungs were no better than his kidneys, but his liver was doing pretty well. Dr. Lilly would say that you needed two out of the three to survive.

Dr. Lilly continued to put everything that he had into The Big Guy's recovery, but nothing was sticking. In the middle of February the decision was made to send The Big Guy back to surgery to work on his lungs. It was thought that with surgery they could remove what the doctors referred to as orange peel so that the lungs could grow and help The Big Guy's breathing. The surgery took four hours and was hailed as a success. Unfortunately, it did not help his breathing numbers and he stayed on the ventilator. Battles won were followed by battles lost, the days kept passing, and my dad was getting tired. At least once a week, someone would say, "This is an amazing man. At his age to have survived through all of this is amazing." He kept fighting, but he was getting tired.

CHAPTER 9

Frustration

It was toward the end of February that I could sense the growing frustration in The Big Guy. Even though he could not talk, nor could he point at letters, I could feel what he wanted. I had known him for forty-six years, and I could see that he had come to the conclusion that he was either not going to make it, or that if he did make it the quality of his life would not be what he was interested in. I thought about the conversation that he and I had had some twenty years earlier on Gorham Street in Madison during a run. My job was to pull the plug if he could not lead a quality life. That story kept coming back to me.

More and more when I saw him, I knew what he was telling me. *I have fought the good fight. I have been here for over two months, and I am not getting better. My kidneys don't work and they never will. My lungs don't work and they are not going to get better. I am not going to leave the hospital only to sit in some room on a ventilator for the rest of my life and be hooked up to a dialysis machine three times a week for four hours at a crack. What the hell are you doing, JB? I told you twenty years ago on that run to pull the plug. Pull the damn plug!*

This sense of frustration started to grow by the day as

February turned into March. Yet I held out hope because my dad had faced many challenges in his life and he had always come out on top. I held out hope that every day that he lived bought the doctors time to figure out the riddle. As his frustration level with me increased, I thought it best if I left for a few days, and so I headed off to Europe for a round of customer meetings.

It was a good break. I spent a day meeting with Trek managers and customers in London. That night with the Trek crew we had beers and dinner and more beers. Physically I was away from my dad, but mentally that was all I really thought about. After dinner I returned to my room to find a missed call from Camille. I called and she told me that Dr. Lilly had discovered a hole in The Big Guy's heart and that this could be what had been holding back his recovery. He could not survive another major surgery, but there was a surgery that they used on infants to plug holes in hearts, and they thought that it might have a chance with The Big Guy. I needed to get home as soon as possible.

The next morning at 5 a.m. I brought together our group of six managers from Trek in the hotel lobby as we prepared to fly on to Amsterdam. I told them that I would be flying home to the United States to be with The Big Guy. As I spoke to the group I could see the concern in their eyes. Just like everyone else, they all figured that in the end he would be fine. This was the first time inside the company that people thought the end might be near.

CHAPTER 10

The Silver Bullet

I flew back to the US and went directly to the hospital. We met with Dr. Lilly and two doctors he had brought in from Children's Hospital. They explained that this could be the silver bullet needed to get him off the ventilator. They clearly stated that this was a fifty-fifty deal at best and that something serious could go wrong. If we decided to go ahead they would bring the equipment over from Children's Hospital because The Big Guy would not survive a move. If something went wrong with the experimental surgery, they would have an additional operating room ready, with surgeons standing by.

The next step was to talk to The Big Guy to see if he was up for this. And so, I went to have a hard conversation with him like I had done so many other times in my life. To tell him that I got a D in science, that I crashed my bike, that I had run out of money, that we missed the sales number. Now I had that same feeling. As I talked to him he was very alert and he clearly let me know that *yes, let's move ahead*. But if this did not work he was finished.

The surgery was planned for the next morning. This was the most optimistic we had been since the day that he woke up and was able to write. Operation Silver Bullet, a surgery that was only used on infants, to save the seventy-three-year-old Big Guy. Perfect. The tide was about to turn. Since The Big Guy had been in the hospital I had been sending out an e-mail update every once in a while. As I went home that night I decided to call in a few favors. My dad was a very blessed man, but he also had done so much for so many. Always doing so without being asked, and never asking for anything in return. For this surgery I figured it would be a good thing to call in a few chips and rally the troops. I sent out the following e-mail:

From: Burke, John
Sent: Wed 2/27/2008 9:17 AM
To: Group = All (includes Int'l Subs)
Subject: Dick Burke update. I need a Favor

Friends of RAB,

As you know, Dick Burke has been in the ICU at Froedtert for the last 70 days recovering from a couple of major heart surgeries. He was making some progress, but his doctors recently discovered that his new heart valve was leaking. It was decided to do a less invasive procedure this week to patch the leak in his heart. At the time, we were looking at a low risk, potentially high return procedure.

In the last four days, my father's condition has deteriorated and the procedure to patch the leak in his heart has increased in importance. The Medical Staff at Froedtert have worked every angle on his case. The procedure to patch The Big Guy's

heart will take place at noon Central Standard
Time. While the procedure is complex, it only takes
thirty minutes. If the procedure fails, the operating
room will be on stand-by for another major heart
surgery. This would be the third major heart surgery
in the last three months, and his ability to survive
another surgery at this point in time is questionable.

My dad likes to send letters to his kids. Yellow
legal pad with the names of the kids in the upper
right. Starts with Kathy (the oldest) and goes all
the way down to Michele (the youngest). A special
red check next to your name for the note that you
receive. Sometime in the fall before all of this mess,
he sent out a short note: "Some light reading that
you might find interesting as you reflect on life."
Along with the note came a book, *This I Believe: The
Personal Philosophies of Remarkable Men and Women.*
As I looked through the book tonight, I came to the
conclusion that the Most Remarkable Person that I
know is my dad. He has done so much for so many of
us, never asking for anything in return.

Today at noon Central Time, we ask you to think
about The Big Guy. We need a Big Day. For the last
seventy-some-odd days he has not drawn very many
good cards. There are not too many left in the deck,
and I am thinking they are all good ones. At noon
say a prayer for The Big Guy, think of your favorite
Big Guy story, get the positive MOJO going.

As for me, I will be waking up early. I am going
for a run as he would want me to. When I come

upon a hill I will pick up the pace as he would. He always loved the hills. When I get home, I will put on the sweater he gave me a few months back. Size Medium, but it really is an extra large. Must have been the wrong label. I will travel down to Milwaukee the city that he loves and has done so much for, and to Marquette the school that he loves. I will walk the grounds with his grandson and then off to the hospital where I will meet up with the rest of the family for Game Day.

My dad always liked it when the chips were down. It always brought out the absolute best in him. Thank you so much for all of your thoughts and prayers over the last few months.

The Burke Family

That morning I did wake up early and I did go for a run. The Big Guy loved to run and so I went on a run for him that morning. He loved the hills and that morning when I hit the hills I ran hard for him. He always picked up the pace on the hills. It always bugged me when he did that, but on this morning I just smiled. Although he wasn't there, he ran with me. After the run, I got in the car and I drove down to Marquette. A decade ago he set up a program called the Burke Scholars, which gave away ten full scholarships a year, plus expenses, in return for twenty hours of community service a week. What I could never figure out is why did my dad fund a program that he himself could never have gotten into? What was he doing for the C students? I made it down to Marquette and I met my son, Richie, at the business school, where there is a plaque in honor of The Big Guy. We checked out the plaque and then we walked around the campus. I then got in the car and headed off to the hospital for game day.

This was it, I was sure that today the tide would turn. I spent time with him before they wheeled him out for surgery. While I was optimistic that the surgery would be a success, I was also realistic that this might be the last time that I would ever see him alive. I had my BlackBerry with me and the e-mails were just rolling in from my request to friends for the Big Guy rally. It was working—people prayed, people went to church, people went for runs, The mojo was flowing, and as he was rolled off to surgery he squeezed my hand. He was very alert and looked very confident.

The surgery did not take the advertised thirty minutes; it took closer to fifteen. It was fast and it was a triumph. The doctors came out and deemed it a complete success. The hole was larger than they had thought, but they plugged it, they were confident. As a family we were so happy. The tide had turned. That day I sent out the following note to The Big Guy's supporters:

February 27, 2008

RAB Friends,

Last night we asked for a favor. We asked that at noon today you pray for The Big Guy, think about The Big Guy, or just get the MOJO flowing for him.

What an incredible response. We had a family who said they would tape their ankles to be ready for game time, we had Father Bill storming the heavens, we had The Big Guy's Secretary forever, Mo Haines, work her magic, we had a Seven Time Winner of a Little Bike Race in France send his best. We had friends praying in Minneapolis, and Washington, DC, we had Trek people around the world rallying for The Big Guy.

I was in The Big Guy's room at around 10 a.m., and he was doing OK. As the emails poured in, I read them to him. For some he would open his eyes, for others, he would smile. As the time got closer to noon I could feel the MOJO in the room. As time got closer for him to leave for the operating room he became much awake and he had a very determined look. As they wheeled him out of the room I held his hand and told him Game Time. He squeezed my hand hard and gave me the nod and off he went.

Today was really an all or nothing deal. The procedure turned out to be "A complete success." The leak in the heart was larger than originally thought, but the plugging of the leak was complete and there was no infection. For sure, he has a long way to go and many obstacles to overcome, but for a guy who has had one setback after another, today was a HUGE day.

On behalf of a very grateful family thank you for all of your support.

It was truly amazing!!!

Thank You.
The Burke Family

There was optimism in the air. For the first time in a long time there was good news. The hole in the heart was plugged. The Big Guy would now be able to do a better job of breathing. Eventually, he would be able to come off the respirator and he would be able to get stronger. Two big open issues remained: would his kidneys come back and would his lungs recover? Only time would tell, but we were heading in the right direction.

CHAPTER 11

The Decision

Over the next few days The Big Guy showed some improvement, but not a lot. We were looking for more and apparently he was, too. My dad had always been able to see a few more steps down the checkers board than anyone else. He had fought the good fight for eighty-plus days and instead of being lifted by the heart surgery, he seemed to know in his own mind that this was the end. When he looked down the checkers board he was not going to be able to make it. He had come to the conclusion that his chances of getting out of the hospital were limited, and that even if he did make it out, he would spend the rest of his life on a breathing machine and would be hooked up to a dialysis machine three days a week.

A week after the surgery, in his own way, he asked me to stop the suffering and withdraw the life support. At first I thought he was being too quick. The family gathered as we had just about every week to hear from the doctors. What were his chances of living? If he lived, what were his chances of having to be hooked up to a breathing machine? If he lived, what were the chances that he would have to undergo dialysis for the rest of his life? We went through all the questions just like Dick Burke would have gone through them all. On a scale of one to ten. The answers came back. Chances of living: five; chances that he would require assisted breathing for at least a few years: nine; chances that he would need dialysis three times a week for four hours at a crack: that one was a ten. I had done my best to spend as much time with him as possible, and I had also done my best to avoid communicating with him about the end of his life. By avoiding the topic, I felt I was buying time. But this was his life, and like everything else in his life, he liked to make the decisions.

On Friday, March 7, late in the afternoon, we brought in an old family friend who was a priest as well as a hospice worker. He had seen this movie before. He met with my father and then he met with us. His message was simple—it was time for The Big Guy to die. That was what he wanted. The entire family was there, and as it should have been it was a family decision. I kept thinking back to the run in Madison some twenty years ago, and his wishes had been clear. In a very weird way, the conversation shifted to when the life support should be withdrawn. Did he want to say good-bye to certain friends before it was over?

Later in the afternoon, I walked out of the conference room on the third floor and headed into the ICU to ask my dad when he wanted to die. I walked into his room, and I asked him if he wanted the life support removed, and he nodded yes. I asked him if he was sure, and he confirmed with another nod. I told him the story of our run in Madison twenty years earlier and I apologized to him for not acting sooner, and explained that I loved him so much and I wanted to make sure that he was given every chance. I told him that he had fought like a warrior and that he had made all of us proud. I then asked him about the timing, and I suggested to him that over the weekend he say good-bye to some close friends and family. And then on Monday he should go. He nodded. I got out my list of names—there must have been twenty-five—and I went through the list. . . . *Would you like to see Joe Siefkes?* Nod yes. I checked it off. *Would you like to see Joel Quadracci?* Nod yes, and I checked it off. We finally got to the end of the list and a schedule was set up for people to come and say good-bye.

We gathered as a family and I let people know whom he would see and whom he would not. We divided the yeses and started to make the phone calls. This proved to be difficult. I remember calling Joe Siefkes, the CFO at Trek who had worked alongside my dad for twenty years. "Joe, I just wanted to give you a call and let you know that The Big Guy is not going to make it. He is going to say good-bye to a few very close friends, and he would like to say good-bye to you." It was a Saturday morning and Joe was shopping for a car and he just broke down.

My dad always referred to life as a journey, and now at journey's end, The Big Guy once again was taking control. The legend was saying good-bye. It was an amazing weekend as the few came from near and far to say good-bye to The Big Guy. Father Bill was around for the weekend, in charge of the spiritual side of this event. The Big Guy's original partner, Red Schmalzer, who was in his mid-eighties, came in from Florida. Over the years the two of them had made a great team. In the mid-1970s when The Big Guy wanted to start Trek, Red was supportive; when

Trek fell on hard times, Red always backed The Big Guy even though there were people who wanted Trek sold or shut down.

Red came to Froedtert Hospital that weekend to say good-bye to his old friend. As it had for the last eighty-six days, the cafeteria served as the gathering place. On this weekend it served as the reception area for the parade of visitors who came to say good-bye. I suppose that it was kind of like a living wake. Instead of coming to pay your respect to the family, in this case people came and paid their respect to the person who was dying. It was a great way to end a great life. All weekend long we sat in the cafeteria at Froedtert Hospital with the characters who had filled the story of his life. He said good-bye to Joe Siefkes and Bob Burns from Trek. He said good-bye to John Thielen and to Father Bill. He said good-bye to his old assistant Mo, and he said good-bye to many other special friends. As Sunday came to an end the reality that my father would die the next day started to hit. It was surreal. I was going to drive home and get some sleep only to wake up and come back to the hospital to watch my father die.

CHAPTER 12

Our Final Meeting

*JB and The Big Guy discussing business
at a Trek dealer event.*

I woke up early the next morning. I went out for a run. Somehow I felt more connected to him as I ran that morning. I got home, took a shower, and put on the sweater that he had given me that fall before he got sick. As I had for almost all of the last eighty-seven days, I got in the car and I headed to Froedtert Hospital with Tania. We arrived around nine o'clock. The plan was to pull the plug at 1 p.m. One by one, my sisters visited with my dad. The tears were flowing as each of my sisters came from his room and joined us as we camped out in the hospital cafeteria. We had been there for eighty-eight days now and this would be the last. More importantly, this would be the last time that I would ever see The Big Guy. I had spent my whole life with him. Almost every big moment of my life had some connection to The Big Guy, and now it was coming to an end.

I wanted my last meeting with The Big Guy to be a good one, so I spent some time preparing for it the night before. He was a bullet-point guy and so was I. He liked lists and so did I. And so, for our final meeting, I put together a list of our top twenty memories. I thought that would be the best way to say good-bye. I also brought along some music for the event. He had an iPod set up in his room with his favorite music that Michele had loaded early in his stay. I brought along the Irish music that we used to listen to when playing Ping-Pong.

I made my way as I had so many times before from the basement cafeteria at Froedtert. Out the door and to the right. Into the elevator and hit floor three. Out the door and into the ICU. There was a button to push, and they would ask your name. John Burke to see Dick Burke. I had been up to the room earlier in the morning, but when I entered again, I was immediately taken by how alert he was. For the man who had gone through four major operations and had spent the better part of almost three months at death's door, this man on his final day and in his final hours looked better than he had for almost every one of those eighty-eight days.

I entered his room and there he was. The Big Guy, with a big smile. He was still hooked up to all of the life-support systems, with a tube stuck down his throat. He was happy that I was there, and I could tell that the order of the day was Be Strong. I couldn't. There were tears flowing down my cheeks as I said to him, "Are you sure that this is the end?" The affirmative nod came with a "Yes, this is, don't fight me anymore" look. I said, "Okay, I just wanted to be sure; you look so good today." He had summoned all of his strength for his final hours. I told him that he was my hero and that I wanted to spend some time going over our top twenty memories. JB and The Big Guy. He smiled. He liked that game. I went to put in the Irish music but I just could not pull the trigger. Too many tears, and the Irish music just would have made it worse.

"Okay, Big Guy, here we go. The top twenty—you and me." He was still smiling. I began . . .

■ Memory #1. Saving My Life

"Dad, do you remember when I was around five and we were in Door County with the Seiberlichs? Peter and I were swimming, and you and Mr. Seiberlich were in this big boat. Mr. Seiberlich moved the boat and the current pulled me under. You knew something was wrong and you dove into the water and pulled me to the top. You never said a word about it but I will always remember that moment."

■ Memory #2. Michele, the Kiltie, and the Turtle

"Dad, do you remember when we used to go to the Kiltie for ice cream on warm summer nights?" The Big Guy's tradition of going to the Kiltie was always the same.

Drive to the Kiltie, order a small ice cream, and drive home. However, on this night, history changed when my sister Michele, the youngest child, broke the string of 2,415 straight small ice creams and ordered the mack daddy—the Turtle Sundae. Michele did not ask permission, she just threw a fastball right across the plate from the backseat . . . "Turtle sundae for me." The Big Guy had been stunned. The Big Guy loved his family and had a very hard time saying no to the youngest two girls, Sharon and Michele.

"Dad, I thought you were going to shoot that one down right away, but you caved and it was a historic moment in the Burke family because it ushered in what my two older sisters and I refer to as the Platinum Program for Sharon and Michele." He smiled.

■ **Memory #3. Sussex Plastics**

"Dad, do you remember when I came home after the first night of work at Sussex Plastics?" I could feel a sense of pride in him as I told this story. I was working at Sussex Plastics the summer of my sophomore year in college. I was working third shift on the plastics line that made the caps reading "Season's Greetings" for the Christmas candy canes that would be filled with M&M's. I came home after the first night of work and was getting something to eat in the kitchen. The Big Guy walked into the kitchen and asked me how my first night of work had gone as he poured a cup of coffee. I responded that it was terrible. The plastic was hot and the gloves had holes, and the plastic burned my hands. "Dad, it's horrible, I am going to quit." I will never forget this as long as I live. He was at the coffee pot and just turned around and looked at me across the room and said, "You will be working at Sussex Plastics all summer long and you will enjoy it." That was it, no yelling or screaming, just one simple statement and he walked out.

The Big Guy had a way of making a big statement with few words. Sussex Plastics was a defining moment in my working career. My dad grew up working summers in a grain elevator and he knew that Sussex Plastics was the best place for me. After The Big Guy gave me a needed attitude adjustment, I ended up working at Sussex Plastics all summer long, and it was by far the best work experience that I ever had to that point in time. Every night I kept a scorecard of how many Season's Greetings caps I could produce per hour. By the end of the summer I held the self-appointed record.

■ **Memory #4. Colorado Bike Trip**

"Dad, do you remember the tunnel?" He nodded his head and managed a huge smile. My dad passed down to me a sense of adventure and doing great things. The summer of my sophomore year in college my dad wanted to take me on a bike trip out West. He had talked about riding from Oregon to Denver. There was a Bikecentennial trail that went across the United States, and he wanted to do the western portion of the trail. He was a busy person and he had set aside two weeks for the trip. As the trip got closer it went from a two-week trip, to a one-week trip, to a let's-drive-out-to-Aspen-and-we-will-go-on-a-three-day trip, all the way down to a two-day trip. We drove from

*The Big Guy and JB at the top of Independence Pass
in 1982 during a bicycle trip around Colorado.*

Wisconsin out to Aspen, and The Big Guy had decided
that we would ride from Aspen to Glenwood Springs, over
to Vail and then up Tennessee Pass to Leadville, and then
down to Twin Lakes, up over Independence Pass, and then
back to Aspen. The highlight of the ride came right outside
of Glenwood Springs, where The Big Guy had us riding on
I-70, the major highway, for about five miles. I kid you not!

There was no shoulder as we rode into the tunnel. About
halfway through the tunnel I could hear a roar that sounded
like a freight train coming right at us. I turned around and
saw a big semi headed right for us with a car coming the
other way. With no shoulder, we got as close as we could
to the side of the tunnel and just hoped like hell that the

semi would not hit us. The sound increased as the semi got closer and I just hung on for my life. Luckily we were both still alive when the semi passed. Turns out it was a Coors beer truck. As soon as it passed, The Big Guy said, "Let's get the hell out of here," and we rode as fast as we could to get out of the tunnel. Once out of the tunnel we still had another four miles on I-70. We made it. That day we rode to Eagle, then on to Leadville, where we stopped for dinner and a beer, and then we rode to Twin Lakes, where we stayed for the night. The next morning was beautiful and we rode our bikes to the top of Independence Pass. At the top, we posed for a picture. "Dad, that is my favorite picture and it hangs in my office."

■ **Memory #5. Playing Tennis**

"Dad, memory number five is playing tennis with you." Everyone hated to play tennis against him. Not only was he a lefty, but he was a master hacker. Big slice backhand and a mean slice with the forehand. He had so much junk that it drove people nuts. "Dad, my favorite tennis memory is the year that you and I played the Morrises in the adult junior final. I can still remember when you turned the Ping-Pong table into a mock tennis court and went over the strategy with me. Remember how the match ended? The Morrises won the first set, we won the second, and it was a tiebreaker in the third. It was 4–4 (9-point tiebreakers in the old days), and Andy served to you; you hit a forehand down the alley toward Missy, it was clear that the ball was going to be wide by about a foot, and then all of a sudden, the ball hit the net and went right over Missy's racquet and into the court. We win!"

■ **Memory #6. Our First Triathlon**

"Dad, do you remember our first and only triathlon?" For some reason, he and I decided to do a triathlon in the early eighties. It must have been one of the first triathlons ever held in the state of Wisconsin. "It was in Madison. What I remember was the swim. You were a terrible swimmer and we were in this lake with a bunch of people and you were not doing so well in the water. I was afraid on the second lap that you were going to drown." Even though I thought The Big Guy would never make it out of the water, he did. He never quit at anything.

"The only other thing that I remember was that after we got out of the water, you did well on the bike and then you were rocking on the run. You did so well on the run that I could barely keep up with you."

■ **Memory #7. The Guy in the Orange Shorts**

To this day, whether I am running or I am on the bike, at some point, I start to pick up the pace and I always remember the guy in the orange shorts. My junior year in high school, The Big Guy decided to go back to school. Off the family went to Boston, where we stayed for the year. In the spring The Big Guy suggested that we sign up for a running race in Cambridge. It was a run along both sides of the Charles River and was 7.5 miles, which was a big deal for

*The Big Guy running in the Mayfair
Half Marathon.*

me. With two miles to go, we were both feeling pretty good when The Big Guy spotted a tall guy about two hundred yards ahead wearing bright orange shorts. "Let's catch the guy in the orange shorts." So we took off after the guy in the orange shorts. We were running pretty fast and we were not closing on him. In disbelief, The Big Guy said, "Let's pick up the pace," which we did as we passed the one-mile-to-go marker, but the guy in the orange shorts was no closer. It was not to be, and we never saw him again. For the next thirty years, whenever we were out running, The Big Guy would always say with a couple of miles left, "Let's catch the guy in the orange shorts," and we would pick up the pace.

■ **Memory #8. Giving Me a Chance at Trek**

The Big Guy had one family business rule: Your last name got you a job at the company. From then on you were on your own. I had joined the company right out of college in May 1984, just as the company was growing like a weed, and I had done pretty well working as a sales rep in the Rocky Mountain states. On almost the day I joined, the company started to have major problems. Trek didn't like the customers, and the customers didn't like Trek. Quality problems, product problems, service issues, the list went on and on. In early 1986 with losses mounting my father replaced the management and took it over himself.

"Dad . . . I will always remember the phone call. I was out in San Francisco visiting customers and I was in my hotel room and you called. You never called when I was on the road. You told me to cut the trip short and return home. I did that and we met at the Nau-Ti-Gal for lunch in Madison. You asked me what I would do if you put me in charge of all the sales and marketing. I gave you my five-minute plan and you said that you were going to make the change on Monday morning. That was it, Dad—you put me in charge of sales and marketing at Trek at age twenty-four." That was my big break. Along with me came Pat Sullivan, Dick Moran, and Giovanna. None of us was over twenty-five, and The Big Guy put us in charge of moving the company forward. He called us the Cub Scouts and we got the job done.

"Dad, do you remember that first meeting with you and me and Sully?" He smiled. Sully was my right-hand man and The Big Guy wanted to know what our sales plan was going to be for the upcoming year. With all the problems at Trek, our dealer base had plummeted from 850 in 1985 to around 450 in 1987. Toward the end of the meeting, as the discussion focused on a new dealer program that we were launching, The Big Guy looked over at Sully and asked, "Pat, how many dealers do you think we will have at the end of the year?" Before I could kick Sully under the table, he blurted out the *big* number that we had been talking about. "We will have a thousand!" Sully has been known to be a bit optimistic at times, and The Big Guy loved to nail people down to commitments. "Pat, are you really going to have a thousand retailers?" Yes. To which The Big Guy replied, "Sully, if you get up to a thousand retailers, I will build a statue of you out in front of the building." Sully, who drinks a lot of coffee, responded with, "Will the stairs go all the way up to the coffee cup?" We ended that year with 1,060 retailers. Trek sales doubled and we were off to the races. The statue idea never came to life, but The Big Guy named the field where we played football every Friday after Pat. The plaque remains today, "Sullivan Field."

- **Memory #9. The Boston Marathon**

"Dad, do you remember when we did the Boston Marathon?" This one made him really smile. He had started running in the mid-seventies and he ran until the end of his life. He loved to run. His dream was always to run in the Boston Marathon, but he never qualified. I think he got within ten minutes one year. He always loved to run with me and so I thought the perfect Christmas gift was

*The Big Guy and JB at the Boston Marathon in 1992,
the year The Big Guy dropped JB on Heartbreak Hill.*

to run the Boston Marathon with him. I knew someone
who could get us in, and for Christmas I told him that
we would run Boston together. He was thrilled! I had not
done any training and the race was less than four months
away. We had a good time getting ready for the race. The
Big Guy would drive up to Madison on Saturdays and he
and I would go out for long runs. They started with a six-
mile run and we built up to doing sixteen-mile runs. Our
final training run was twenty miles.

We headed off to Boston on the Friday before the race
and had a great time eating and drinking at some of our
favorite spots. We took the rental car and drove the Boston
Marathon course. He always wanted to be prepared. The
morning of the race we boarded a school bus and headed for

Hopkinton. We got there three hours before race time and hung around Hopkinton High. As race time approached we walked from the high school to downtown Hopkinton and stood with ten thousand other runners waiting for noon on Patriots' Day to begin the race into Boston. About five minutes before noon, the Hopkinton High band played "The Star-Spangled Banner." It was as if we were playing in the Super Bowl. We were both pretty excited.

As the gun went off, it took us about eight minutes just to get to the starting line, and then we were off, down a hill past some houses. I can still hear someone's stereo playing "Eye of the Tiger" as we passed by. It was a crisp, beautiful day. We went through Ashland and Framingham and Natick and I was feeling pretty good. "Dad, do you remember Wellesley?" All of the girls from Wellesley College were out on the road. It was a tunnel of women for around six hundred yards. There was an older guy in front of me and when we finished getting through the tunnel he said to me, "I am going to go back and do that again!" He did. The Big Guy's eyes lit up. We passed the halfway point in good shape and headed to Newton. A nice downhill into Newton and then there was a ninety-degree turn at the firehouse, and there it was: "Heartbreak Hill." We started up the hill together and it was clear at this time that my fifty-five-year-old father had more in the tank than his twenty-eight-year-old son. Someone handed me an orange slice and I fumbled it and it went over my head. I reached around and caught the slice behind my back. The crowd went wild! Catching an orange behind my back was the highlight of my marathon.

Heartbreak Hill is made up of three hills, and at about

83

the halfway marker, The Big Guy took off. Gone. What happened to the father-son event? I just chuckled as he flew up the hill. I was glad to see him go because I did not want to hold him back anymore. "Dad, you were flying that day." He gave me one of those "Are you kidding me?" looks. I managed to pull it together and finished. "Dad, do you remember how tired I was?" He nodded. I was only able to consume two beers that night, and the next morning they almost had to get a wheelchair out to get me on the plane.

We ended up running Boston three times. After the second time he presented me with a framed piece that had three pictures of him and me, along with a note dated April 16, 1990, and April 15, 1991. It read: "John, Thanks for coming along on two of the greatest trips of my life. May we have the opportunity to ride the Bus and climb the Hill many more times. The Journey was certainly the Goal. Love D."

"Dad, you know that those were three of the best days of my life. I have always hung that piece in a special place and will never forget the three Bostons that we ran together."

The Big Guy's love of running was passed on to me. I continue to run to this day and in 2010 I asked my son to run with me in the New York City Marathon as my Christmas gift. We ended up running that race as a tribute to my dad, but more importantly the lesson of physical fitness and doing great things was passed on from one generation to the next.

■ **Memory #10. Your Letters**

"Dad, one of my favorite memories and number ten on my list are all of the letters that you sent to me. My handwriting is the worst and yours is the *best*." I once asked you why. "That's easy—I went to a Catholic grade school and if the nuns did not like your handwriting they would rap your knuckles with a ruler. Very motivational!" His letters would always include a family update, a weather update (he hated the winter), and a business update (business was always slow; you would never believe that this man built a great business by reading his letters!). Later in life when all of his kids were on their own, he would send out updates on the business, and even updates on his personal life. He would have the names of his five kids on the top left of the memo, and put a red check next to your name.

"You know, Dad, I read all of your letters, and I have kept most of them! They bring back some of the very best memories."

- **Memory #11. Father Bill and the Nativity Jesuit Middle School**
One of The Big Guy's great legacies is giving back to people under the radar screen. No names on buildings, no big portraits or parades. Just do what you are supposed to do. He was a little bit surprised by this one. I was at a Marquette University event and Father Bill came up and introduced himself; it must have been fifteen years ago. We talked for a few minutes. I'm thinking, *Dad, Father Bill likes you. Another one of your friends!* "Anyways, after telling a few stories Father Bill thanks me for all that our family had done for the Nativity Jesuit Middle School. I asked Father Bill what you had done for the school and he told

me that you had paid for a big part of the tuition for the one hundred and twenty boys who went to school there. I thought that was pretty cool. But what was really cool was that I did not know this, and neither did anyone else."

The Big Guy did so many great things for people and he never blew his horn. He went on to be the major donor for the Urban Ecology Center in a poor part of town near a lousy park on a polluted river. The new center now serves over seventy thousand kids a year from the inner cities who do not have the chance to get out to the country. It also serves as a community center on those cold days when kids have nowhere to go. He did other things, like being the major donor for construction of the Milwaukee Youth Arts

The Big Guy at the Urban Ecology Center in Milwaukee.
His donation to build the building bought the un-naming rights.

Center. He donated all this money on one condition. He purchased the un-naming rights, so that his name would not appear on any building. "Dad, you did so much for so many people. I am so proud of you."

■ **Memory #12. Your Speech at the First Trek World**

I had this idea after reading a book that we should invite all of our customers to Wisconsin for a three-day mini trade show. It was *awesome*. It was 1989 and Trek had turned the corner. Dealers who used to hate Trek loved Trek. The product was good, dealers were getting awesome service, the marketing was right, and we were on a roll. Dealers came in on Friday night and we hosted a great cocktail party. The anticipation to see the new product was very high. The next morning the dealers saw the product and they loved it! Fish were jumping into the boat. It was incredible. That night we had an awards banquet and we handed out awards to our customers—it was an all-time high. Our featured speaker of the night followed the awards, and I had the honor of introducing The Big Guy.

The Big Guy started to talk about the history of Trek. He took it right up to 1986 and said that at that time the company had almost gone bankrupt and it was on the ropes. I could not believe my ears. He went on to tell the crowd that he had tried to sell the company but that no one would buy it. He thought about closing it down but that was too expensive. Customer enthusiasm was at its peak, and now The Big Guy was telling the customers how bad things had been at Trek. I remember leaning over to Sully

*A frustrated JB serving beer after The Big Guy's
famous inaugural Trek World speech.*

and saying, "ten," then "twenty." When Sully asked what I was doing, I said, "I'm counting the thousands of bike sales that we are losing as this speech goes on." I couldn't believe it.

As he always did when he finished, The Big Guy turned around and looked at me and said, "How was that?" I looked him straight in the eye and said, "That was terrible!" I walked off the stage on my way to Casino Night and ran into twenty customers along the way who pulled me aside and told me that was the best speech they ever heard. I heard from just about everyone that at one point in time

88

they had almost lost it all and that my dad was so honest and humble and they really appreciated that.

The Big Guy was a great speaker and one of his greatest attributes was the brutal truth. He almost liked shocking the audience with it.

■ **Memory #13. Not Firing Me from Trek**

The Big Guy was all about loyalty. He would put loyalty ahead of just about anything. There is a reason why most of the people who worked with The Big Guy spent their entire careers with him.

At Trek, 1996 was not a good year and 1997 was not going much better. In the spring of 1997, The Big Guy promoted me to president of Trek. It was a bad year, and 1998 was worse. We were making a lot of changes to turn the business around, but it was bad. The board wasn't happy, the banks weren't happy, and The Big Guy wasn't all that happy, either. There was pressure to sell the company or to remove me. The Big Guy told me during the storm that he would stick by me and he knew that we would pull through. "Dad, we ended up pulling through and created the best bicycle company in the world. I will never forget your loyalty during the tough times."

■ **Memory #14. Your Speech at the Marquette Alumnus of the Year Luncheon**

"Dad, I remember one day we were on a run and you told me that you really didn't like awards. But the one award that you would like to win was the Marquette Alumnus of the Year." I knew why. My dad graduated from high school and went to college, and after the first week he figured out that the college was not for him. He returned home and his mother took matters into her own hands and took my dad down to see the priest to set him straight. The priest made a phone call and the next day my dad was enrolled at Marquette University. My dad loved Marquette. He was successful at life but he was not a very successful student. He was your typical C student. Sure enough, a couple of years after our talk, my dad was awarded the prestigious award of Marquette Alumnus of the Year. I went to the awards luncheon and he gave what I considered to be one of his finest speeches. In front of the university president and distinguished faculty and alumni, the C student from Elmhurst gave an incredible talk. He told the story of how he got into Marquette and he took people through the life of a C student. Most importantly he told the audience about the chance in life that Marquette had given him and all of the life lessons that his four years at Marquette had taught him. "Dad, I was so proud of you that day, you spoke for all the C students in the world and you did it very well."

- **Memory #15. The 1999 Tour de France**

"Dad, remember the 1999 Tour?" He loved to tell the story.

My dad was an accountant by trade who got his start working as a credit manager at Caterpillar. He did not like to spend money, let alone marketing money, on a bike racing team. It was 1998 when we were in the midst of our money-losing streak at Trek, and we were sponsoring the Saturn racing team in the United States. One day Dick Moran, our marketing manager, walked into my office and said, "How would you like to sponsor the Postal Service team? They are going to form a new team."

"How much money is it going to cost us above the Saturn team?" I asked.

"An extra hundred thousand dollars for a total of two hundred and fifty thousand dollars and then we need to sign a contract with Lance Armstrong for a hundred thousand dollars."

"Who's he?" I replied.

"He won the world championships a few years ago, got cancer, and now he's coming back."

"Okay, do it."

That was it. The conversation lasted less than a minute. Some people say that luck plays a role in business. They are correct.

The biggest issue we had was that Trek did not make a time trial bike. The first stage of the 1999 tour was a short time trial. Lance ended up winning the race and was the first American to wear the yellow jersey since Greg LeMond. The first American ever to wear the jersey riding an American bike. Spirits were running high at Trek although no one—and I mean *no one*—ever thought he would win the race.

The race continued and Lance was doing really well, probably top five before the mountains. The first big stage in the mountains was a race that finished on the top of

Sestriere. Dick Moran was in France monitoring the race for Trek. I get a call from Dick from a phone booth. "You're not going to believe this, but he won the race up Sestriere and now he is three minutes ahead in the yellow jersey. He could win this thing." Holy shit. I get on the phone. "Big Guy, you're not going to believe this one, but Lance won the race today up Sestriere. He is in front by three minutes. Moran says that he could win this thing." My dad replies, "Holy shit!" I continue, "Moran said that someone should get over there. I have a few problems on the home front, so why don't you get on a plane and head on over there?" He made it to Paris on Friday afternoon. There was a pivotal time trial on Saturday and then the traditional race into Paris on Sunday. Saturday's time trial would determine the winner. "Dad, do you remember where you watched the time trial from?" His eyes lit up. He rode in the team car with the team director, Johan Bruyneel, directly behind Lance. It was a one-hour time trial winding through the small towns in France. Johan had The Big Guy run the clock and keep track of the splits. The Big Guy loved it. Lance won the time trial and was in perfect position to take a ceremonial ride into Paris the next day.

He called me after the race finished to confirm the good news that Lance Armstrong had won the Tour de France—the biggest bicycle race in the world—on a Trek bike. I knew that it was one of The Big Guy's highlights. As he watched on the Champs-Élysées that Sunday afternoon he got goose bumps as they played "The Star-Spangled Banner." "Dad, do you remember telling me what the concierge at the hotel did when you walked into the hotel after the race?" Big smile, and The Big Guy gave me his signature thumbs-up. Indeed as he walked into the hotel the concierge had given my dad a thumbs-up. My father would say, "I think for that one day even the French loved the Americans."

■ **Memory #16. Building the Best Bicycle Company in the World with You**

"As you always liked to say, Dad, there were bumps along the way . . ." The Big Guy and I did not always see eye to eye when it came to business. He was more organized, a better planner, more cost controlled. He used to love to tell people that I was *ready, fire, aim.* I felt bad about that for a few years until one day I read a book that said that there are two types of people in the world: *ready, fire, aim* and *ready, aim, aim, aim . . .* !

We took a lot of pride in building the business together. Even when I took over as president of the company The Big Guy was there for every big decision. We did not always agree; in fact most of the times we didn't agree. The Big Guy loved to be the great contrarian. If I said black, he would say white; when I said I was tired of the winter, he would talk of his love for the seasons; when I had bad news, he would always find the silver lining in the black cloud. He was at his best when there was a crisis. In 1992, the year that George Soros broke the Bank of England and the dollar plummeted, we were on the wrong side of a big currency bet and lost $8 million. The bankers didn't like it but The Big Guy held firm.

In 1998 when we were losing money, the federal government changed the rules on 401(k) plans, allowing employees to take their money out and switch investments at any time. Good idea. The only problem was that we were having a couple of lousy years, and if Trek employees switched investments, it would be a big drain on the company. To make matters worse this was the time of the roaring stock market and everyone thought a good return was 20 percent.

With their Trek stock declining and the stock market roaring, Joe Siefkes, our CFO, and I met with The Big Guy to let him know of the rule change and our prediction that many employees would take their cash out. I will never forget his reaction. "Are you kidding me? This is a great company with a great future and the stock is cheap. If people want to sell their stock, I will buy every damn share." In the end 80 percent of the employees sold their stock and The Big Guy did buy "every damn share." Over the next ten years Trek stock gained 385 percent in value. "Dad, together we built the *best* bicycle company in the world, and while we did not always agree, we built it together."

■ Memory #17. 2008 New Product Introduction

The year 2006 was not our best year, and I told The Big Guy that we needed to double our spending on product and design to generate best-in-class products. He agreed and that was it. We doubled down, added some really incredible people, and today Trek generates the best products in the world year in and year out. And it is only getting better. In June of 2007 we introduced the first of the

The 2008 Madone launch, a turning point for Trek.

new products to come from the "Double Down Strategy." It was the Madone launch, our premier carbon-fiber road bikes. At the last minute we also decided to introduce the new generation of full-suspension mountain bikes, the Fuel EX. The introduction was held at the Milwaukee Arts Center, and we planned a rehearsal at 4 p.m. with the unveiling scheduled to take place at 6 p.m.

As we kicked off the rehearsal I looked toward the back and saw The Big Guy sitting by himself in the back row. Vintage Big Guy, wearing a sweatshirt and his twenty-year-old Nativity baseball hat. The rehearsal was an absolute bust. It was the worst presentation I had ever seen. I was too busy trying to pick up the pieces to talk to The Big Guy. But we got things worked out, and thirty minutes later we put on what was probably the best presentation in

Trek's history. The introduction was awesome, the product even better. We had turned the corner and it ushered in a new era at Trek. The company with the best customer service in the business was now tooled up to produce the best products in the business.

"Big Guy, do you remember when I saw you after that presentation, you asked me how the hell we pulled that off? You told me that was the worst rehearsal you had ever seen and I agreed." The key, I told him, was *ready, fire, aim*. Two months later he spent a few days visiting customers in the San Francisco area. He came back and he was fired up. They loved the new products, and they loved the marketing. In the middle of August we had our annual sales meeting where The Big Guy always spoke. I had learned my lesson and always gave him three or four bullet points; however, this time, I had no idea what he was going to say. It was in Madison at Breese Stevens Field under a tent, and it would be his last speech. He was a great speaker and this was one of his best. He talked about the past, he talked about the present, and then he focused on the future. He called this year the best year in the history of Trek and said that at no time in its history did Trek have a brighter future. He was right. Trek went on to a series of record years.

"Dad, you are leaving on top." He looked at me and he smiled. He knew that.

■ Memory #18. Showing Up at the Ironman

The first time I participated in Ironman Wisconsin, hosted in my hometown of Madison, The Big Guy was out of town. The second time, in 2006, he was in town but sounded reluctant to make the trip to Madison. At the last minute he decided to come. It was a lousy day. It ended up being fifty-seven degrees, and it poured rain from the time I got out of the water at 8:30 a.m. until we walked across the finish line at just after 9 p.m. As we started out the run, there he was, The Big Guy. I was so glad to see him. I knew he would like the event and I knew that deep down he was proud that I was "getting it done," as he liked to say. The running course went in and around Madison a few times so that the spectators could see the runners six or

The Big Guy showing up at the Madison Ironman to watch JB.

eight times without trying that hard. He worked the course hard, and so we saw him all over the place.

"Dad, do you remember the Ironman?" Once again the big eyes, the head shaking back and forth with a smile. Even though he could not talk I knew exactly what he was saying. *I remember, I was there. You were crazy for doing that, but you know that I was very proud of you.* "Dad, I wanted you to be there because I wanted you to understand what you created. Without you as a role model, I never would have run a marathon, I never would have competed in an Ironman or any of the other goofy events that I do. It all comes from you, Dad." He knew this and he was happy.

■ **Memory #19. The Trek Football Game**

"Dad, do you remember the football game three years ago? You called me on the phone from Florida and asked when the game was going to be. I gave you the date and you showed up at the age of seventy." Every year we have a football game between the Old Guys, made up of the thirty-five-and-older crowd, and the Young Bucks, who are all the guys in the office younger than thirty-five. It is an extremely competitive game usually played in December, under the lights at Firemen's Park in Waterloo. On this evening The Big Guy was stellar. He played offense and caught six passes in what turned out to be the eighteenth straight win for the Old Guys. "Big Guy, everyone was so impressed with your performance."

The Big Guy at age seventy playing in the annual Old Guys vs. Young Bucks football game. He caught six passes in a winning effort.

■ **Memory #20. My Wedding**

I had gotten married to Tania that past August. The Big Guy loved Tania. We had a bike ride that afternoon before the wedding, and during the bike ride I asked him if he would give a toast. I knew what the response would be. "I can't believe that you are asking me three hours before the event." I always asked him to speak late, and he always gave me that line, and he always gave a great speech. It was a beautiful night at the house and we held the ceremony on the patio overlooking the lake. As he addressed the audience he said that I was a total overachiever, and that he and I had had our differences (Wow! For a wedding toast, Big Guy?), but that Tania was spectacular and that we would go far and we would go fast. "Dad, it was a great toast and I will always remember it."

After the toast we had a cocktail party. Later in the evening The Big Guy pulled me aside and we had a nice chat about how awesome the night had been and how great Tania is and how lucky I was. "Dad, do you remember the end of the conversation? I said to you, 'Big Guy, I just want to thank you for everything. Everything I have has come from you.' And you replied, 'John, everything I have has come from you. We have made a great team.' I gave you a big hug and noticed that Dan Titus, Trek's regional sales manager, was standing right there in awe. That was a memorable night."

The Big Guy giving a toast at Tania and JB's wedding.
"They will go far and they will go fast."

CHAPTER 13

Good-bye

The final lesson from The Big Guy.

I had finished with the Top 20 Memories Game, but I had one last thing that I wanted to say to The Big Guy. "Dad, I want to say thank you for having left me and everyone in this family a great last name." He smiled with the tube still down his throat keeping him alive. My dad loved to talk about integrity. He was Mr. Integrity. When he said something would get done, it would. When he said that he believed that people should give back, he led the charge. Always under the radar screen and never seeking to bring attention to himself, his family, or his company. He did things simply because he believed it was the right thing to do.

Now it had come to an end. He asked for the board of letters that he could point at so that he could be understood. He had barely been able to use this during the entire eighty-eight days, but now he summoned all of his strength at this moment. He took the board and pointed to the letters. W I L L T H I N G S C H A N G E A T T R E K?

Here we are at the end and he wants to talk about Trek? Over the last eighty-eight days, I had given him some brief updates on what was happening at the company. He never seemed that interested; he had bigger problems to deal with. But in his last hour of life, his final question for me was: will things change at Trek? I looked at him and I smiled. "Well, Big Guy . . . not that much. Same old thing. Ready, fire, aim." He shook his head.

It was my turn for a question. "Dad, are you sure that you want the plug pulled? I just want to check, one last time." A definitive yes. "Dad, I love you so much." He summoned the board once again. It was like a scene from the movies, and I will never forget it. On second thought, it was better than a scene from the movies. He took the board and asked for a pen. I handed him a Sharpie and he started to circle the letters one at a time. I L O V E Y O U. And then he put his left hand in the air and circled the room. "Dad, do you mean you love everyone?" He nodded yes. "Love you, too, Dad."

It was time for me to go. It was just past noon and the

plug would be pulled at one o'clock. He would spend his last hour with Camille and Father Bill. I gave him one last hug, and with tears streaming down my face I walked out of the room backwards so that I could keep an eye on him. I did not want to let go. I will never forget this as long as I live—he gave me a salute and his usual thumbs-up. I gave him a thumbs-up back and walked out the door.

I returned to the basement of Froedtert Hospital. The family was all there. Everyone talked about his or her last visit with The Big Guy. Their best moments growing up, the impact that he had had on their lives, the things that they were most proud of him for. I was overcome with emotion. It was the most moving experience of my life. It was difficult for me to believe that this great life would come to an end; yet at the same time I was so proud of my dad.

CHAPTER 14

Journey's End

*The Big Guy and friend Gary Johnson
walk Vero Beach.*

A t one o'clock we went back up to the third floor for the last time. We were greeted by the doctors and my dad's head nurse, Fran. Camille was there, too. The doctors explained that he would be taken off the life-support system and would be in as little pain as possible. They expected he would last for eight to ten minutes. This was one of those bizarre moments in life. The Big Guy had requested that Fran be there at the end. Camille asked if anyone else would like to be present when the life support was removed. Although I didn't want to do this, I was not going to miss the final moments of my dad's life. I wanted to be there for him. I remember my sister Michele waffling and I reached back and grabbed her hand and took her along. I figured she probably really wanted to be there, and I needed her to be there.

After the life support was pulled and the machines were taken out of the room, the entire family gathered in his room. There must have been twenty people as we stood and listened to his favorite music. We started telling stories as the minutes ticked by. After ten minutes the doctor came by and said he might last longer, perhaps thirty minutes. We pulled out some of the great letters and cards that had been sent and we read them out loud. Great stories from exceptional people who The Big Guy had touched along the way. It was a very emotional experience. My father would have loved it.

Thirty minutes came and went. He was still going strong. This was vintage Dick Burke. The 5'8" Big Guy, the one underestimated most of his life, was making one last statement. This was his last marathon. He was proving a point. When we hit the hour mark, I said to two of my brothers-in-law, Derek and Jeff, why don't you head out and get some beer? They returned thirty minutes later with a couple of cases of beer to find that The Big Guy was still going strong. The party would last for another few hours. The beer was flowing and so were the stories and the tears. It was an amazing scene.

The time now was six o'clock and The Big Guy who was supposed to last for eight minutes had now lasted for five hours. The room started to empty as people headed for home. I stayed in the room with Tania and Kathy. At seven o'clock I started to pass the time by writing the final note that would go out to his network of friends. Not knowing when he would die, I put in a placeholder at 10:59 . . . The time passed and around 9:30 I fell asleep. Tania and Kathy kept awake with The Big Guy. At 10:55 Tania woke me up to tell me he was going. The Big Guy passed away at exactly 10:59.

It was over. My dad was gone. The great life had come to an end. I had to call the funeral home and make arrangements. Kind of weird. No . . . really weird. I called Camille, and I called other family members to tell them that he had passed. Tania and I left the third floor of Froedtert Hospital, where we had visited over the last eighty-eight days, for the last time. We got in the car and drove home. That night after I got home I sent out the following note:

Friends,

At 10:59 this evening The Big Guy passed away surrounded by family and Father Bill. His body died, his spirit lives on.

Over the past week, his health had been deteriorating and over the weekend he said goodbye to close family and friends. It was Vintage Big Guy. Calling the shots right up until the end. As he faded this afternoon, the doctors gave him 5–10 minutes to live; he lasted over nine hours. Vintage Big Guy. The family gathered and as time went on, we went into our "What would The Big Guy do?" mode, so part of the family was sent out on a beer run and we turned Room 10, 3rd floor ICU at Froedtert Hospital into a celebration of The Big Guy's life. We told Big Guy stories and read many of the cards and letters that have poured in over the last 88 days. We played his favorite tunes from Frank Sinatra, John Denver, and Barbra Streisand. We said good-bye to the Legend.

It's hard to believe that it is over. He fought the good fight.

At his 70th birthday party, The Big Guy gave a memorable speech about his life and how he had planned to do one more great thing. He wasn't sure what it was, but he had a feeling. As the days passed in the hospital and the odds stacked up against him I knew that the great thing would be that he would dance with death and beat it. I was sure of it. I had the party planned.

I was wrong, he did not beat death, but he did do something great. He fought like a warrior, and he died with dignity, class, and honor. He died on his terms. He said good-bye knowing that his wife loved him, his kids loved him, and that he had so many friends all over the world who followed his fight pulling for him all the way. There is a reason that a man five foot eight is called The Big Guy. He was a small man with a very big heart. He leaves behind a great spirit and a legacy that to whom much is given, much is required.

When I said my final good-bye this morning I took him through my Top 20 JB/Big Guy memories (sorted high to low). When I finished he asked for his board. Since he could not talk with breathing support, he would point to letters on the board. He took the pen out of my hand and instead of pointing he circled the letters with a black Sharpie. L. . . . . . . O. . . . . . . V. . . . . . . E space Y. . . . . . . He got back to the O which had already been circled and he circled it again, and then finally. . . . . . U. He then raised his hand and with his finger made a motion circling the room. I said to him, "everyone," and he gave me the nod. It was not only for me, but for the family he loved and for all of the friends who thought and prayed for him over the last three months. A lot of people loved my dad. He loved a lot of people. He had 73 GREAT years and in the final sentence of a note that he left behind he signed off with . . . "Thanks, it was a great ride. Love, d."

Thank you for all of your prayers and support over the last three months. A celebration of a Great Life will take place soon. Details to follow. As we prepare for the Celebration of The Big Guy's life, if you have any great Big Guy Stories please pass them along.

The Burke Family

CHAPTER 15

The Celebration
of a Great Life

*The Big Guy celebrates at the wedding
of Tania and JB.*

I woke up the next morning and went for a run. I was
not mad or angry that he had died. I was proud. I finished the run and headed to work. I did not really want
to see anyone; I just needed something to do. I got to the
office and my e-mail inbox was full with people sending

their condolences and their favorite Big Guy stories. My father's lifelong secretary, Mo Haines, called and said that she had an envelope to be given to me upon his death. I arranged to meet her and had my hopes up that it would be some sort of classic note from The Big Guy covering all the issues that I would face in the coming months and how he wanted everything handled. The note did not contain any great information with the exception that he did not want a funeral, he wanted a celebration. Classic Big Guy.

The family gathered and the decision was made to have a celebration of his life. The date would be St. Patrick's Day. He would love that. The place would be the Milwaukee Youth Arts Center. My dad had given the money to build an arts center for kids living in the roughest part of Milwaukee. It was only fitting that this would be the site of his celebration.

The preparations began. We wanted to make sure the celebration matched the man. We decided that there would be an opener by Father Bill, followed by speakers from different phases of his life, a slide show of his life, and then a celebration to follow. The Big Guy had been a special guest at a bicycle event hosted by Team Active in Michigan the year before, and in his honor they produced "Big Guy Ale" for the event. He loved it. He talked about it so much that I called the person who organized the Michigan event and had them send me two cases. I gave everyone in the family a six-pack and The Big Guy a case. In the Big Guy's honor, we had more Big Guy Ale produced for the celebration, along with his favorite Dairy Queen Blizzards for dessert. My sister Michele had ordered special shamrock ties for the fellas, which my dad would have loved. The night before the celebration the family gathered for dinner at Lainey's house. We had dinner, told Big Guy stories, and finalized preparations for the next day.

The day of the celebration was cold and cloudy, classic Milwaukee weather for mid-March. I arrived at the Youth Arts Center a couple of hours before the visitation began. We had no idea how many people would be there. As the visitation began, the line was long and it kept getting longer over time. There were a lot of people who came by to pay their respects and say good-bye to my dad. However, it wasn't the number of people who showed up—it was the diversity of the crowd. There were employees of Trek, Trek customers had who traveled from all over the country, Trek suppliers from around the world, Marquette University people, people from nonprofits from all over Milwaukee who had benefited from his generosity, business associates, and of course there were so many friends.

The visitation was supposed to end at four o'clock and Father Bill was to begin the celebration at that time. The visitation line was still a few hundred strong and I went down the line to make sure that I thanked everyone for being there. I walked quickly into the auditorium, where Father Bill had already started. I took my seat in the front row next to my son, Richie, and Tania. Father Bill was exceptional. He talked about my dad and the good times that they had had together. He talked about a hike that they had done in Colorado where my father had asked Father Bill to preside at a celebration of his life if he should pass first. Father Bill had agreed. The Big Guy had then told

Father Bill that he was not religious and that he did not believe in God. Father Bill explained that over the eighty-eight days he spent in the hospital The Big Guy had come to believe there was something greater in the universe. On his final day he asked Father Bill to give him the last rites.

Many people told great stories about how my dad had touched their lives. Tony Lo, president of Giant Bicycle, spoke about the special partnership between Trek and Giant. He described their first business meeting—how after Tony had answered all of The Big Guy's questions, The Big Guy shook Tony's hand and said, "I can trust you." He went on to talk about how, under The Big Guy's leadership, Trek grew to become the number one bicycle brand in the world. Yozo Shimano, president of Shimano, was next. Yozo talked about the great relationship between Shimano and Trek—that while Dick Burke was a great businessman he was a far greater person. The last speaker from the bicycle industry was Jay Graves, owner of the Bike Gallery in Portland. The Bike Gallery is a Top 5 Trek retailer. Jay told the story of the day in the early 1980s when Dick Burke visited the Bike Gallery. At that time the Bike Gallery was in bad shape. The timber industry was in bad shape, the bank had just cut the Bike Gallery's credit line, and Jay's father had had to sell their house in order to stay out of foreclosure. Jay and his father met with The Big Guy. At the end of the meeting, with the Bike Gallery being seriously past due to Trek, The Big Guy looked Jay and his father in the eyes and said, "I believe in you and we will work with you." The Bike Gallery recovered and was current with Trek two years later. It went on to become one of Trek's legendary customers.

Joel Quadracci spoke. The Big Guy had known Joel's father, Harry, who was a legend himself. Harry had founded Quad/Graphics, a large and successful printing company, and The Big Guy was a long-serving board member. Five years earlier Harry had died in an accident, and The Big Guy was asked to step in as chairman of the company and help with the transition. Joel talked about how much The Big Guy had done for Quad and then he talked about saying thank you to The Big Guy as well as being able to say good-bye. "I never had the chance to say good-bye to my father. You don't know how much it means to say good-bye to someone." It was a very good point and I was so thankful that I had been able to say good-bye to my dad.

Stephanie Quade, a dean at Marquette who ran the Burke Scholars program, spoke. She told the story of the Burke Scholars—a program that The Big Guy had set up some fifteen years ago that offered a full ride, along with living expenses, to students with service and leadership potential. In return, the students needed to volunteer in the community for twenty hours a week. This has turned out to be the most prestigious scholarship program at Marquette, and more than one hundred students have graduated as Burke Scholars. Stephanie told the story about The Big Guy once arriving early for a meeting and wanting to take a nap. Stephanie found him a room with a couch. "No, that is too nice for me; I will just take a nap over here." The Big Guy took off his jacket, turned it into a pillow, and lay down between two file cabinets. Vintage Big Guy!

Nicole Hurdle, a Burke Scholar, followed Stephanie.

She started out by showing the crowd her lucky socks. "These are the socks I wore the day I met Dick Burke, and when I was accepted into the program I decided that these would be my lucky socks. After my first semester I wrote a note to Dick Burke to give him an update on my progress. Two weeks later, I received a handwritten note back from Dick with some comments and advice. At the end of every semester I wrote Dick a letter, and every time I received one back. Today I am here to say good-bye to a man whose generosity, love, and support for his community have shaped me and hundreds of others. Mr. Burke has been a part of every decision I have made, every place that I have lived, and every step that I have taken in these lucky socks since the day that I met him." Nicole could not have described The Big Guy better.

Then my sister Kathy started by carrying up to the stage the Blarney Stone sign that my father had stolen from a bar in Atlanta some thirty-five years ago. It was so fitting, being St. Patrick's Day.

Kathy said, "When we were young Dad told us that even though he was Irish and our mother was German, if anyone were to ask, tell 'em you are one hundred percent Irish." My sister Mary followed and talked about The Big Guy as a guiding light in her life. As she explained, he was always the first person she sought for advice.

My sister Sharon followed. Earlier in the week I asked her if she wanted to speak at the celebration. "No, I don't really have anything," she replied. A few days later she called and said that she had written something about Dad. It was spectacular and she agreed to speak:

The Celebration of a Great Life

My Dad was:
Frugal, but spared no expense when it came to his kids
Elusive, but always available
Planning travel, but loving home the most
Avoiding a party, the life of the party
Set in his routine, yet up for an adventure
Busy, but not enough
Little on size, big on personality
Humble, but fiercely confident
Inquisitive, but opinionated
Concise with his words, saying a lot without saying a lot
Chocolate, ice cream, coffee, beer, wine, but running,
*   hiking, biking, golf, tennis, and more*
No pictures, loved fame
His telling me on a 1–10 scale, not congruent with the
*   listening he loved to do*
Loved the seasons, hated the winter!

My dad saw the best in people; he would leave his car keys in his car at the airport. That is not clueless, that is unique. Trusting someone before they give you some reason not to sounds simple. The things that he accomplished on a worldly scale are amazing, the people he touched close around him are fortunate, and the ones who love him find comfort and respect in him now and forever.

He called me the #3 daughter, but he let me know in so many ways how special I was to him. I hope everyone who reads this can relate, because then you can accurately know the simple guy he loved to be.

She rocked the house and he would have been so proud of her. I was.

I spoke last. I told the story about the speech he gave at his seventieth birthday party and how he had made two predictions at the end of the speech. The first was that he would live to 2020, and the second was that he had one last great thing to do. Even though his life was cut short and he did not live to 2020, he did achieve that one last great thing. The one last great thing that The Big Guy did was teach us the lessons of life in his last eighty-eight days. I concluded by saying that I would think about him every day for the rest of my life. I would think about him when I was standing over a four-foot putt on the golf course because he would always talk to himself when putting. "Put the ball in the goddamn hole, Dick!" I would think of him whenever I went running. We had run three marathons together and whenever he would hit the base of a hill he would always say, "Let's hit it hard!" I would think of him whenever I saw a Dairy Queen or whenever I stopped at one. He loved a good Blizzard. I said that whenever I saw a Trek bike I would think of the man who never lost faith in his company.

I finished by telling the story that someone had once told me: that his body would die but that his spirit would live on. I thanked everyone for coming, and then, on cue, a slideshow of his life played. A picture is worth a thousand words, and it was really powerful. After the slideshow ended we finished by playing some video that we had dug up in the Trek archives. My two favorites were the start and the end. It started with The Big Guy saying, "It's been a great program and I know you have been sitting on your ass for an hour and a half." The last clip came from a Trek dealer meeting, and in it he looked into the audience and thanked everyone for their business and everything that they had done for Trek. "Without your support we would not be here. As for me, this has been a great ride and I hope to be here for a few more years." As he finished, the camera stayed with him as he walked off the stage, down some steps, and into the darkness.

Every time I think about my dad I am not angry or bitter that he died. I am so proud. I keep going back to his seventieth birthday party and his prediction that he would do one last great thing. In his own mind he believed that the last great thing that he would do would be to give away a massive amount of money and use his business talents to help change the world. He never got that chance but he did do one last great thing. During his last eighty-eight days of life The Big Guy taught those around him the life lessons of humility, giving, courage, dignity, and L-O-V-E.

His spirit lives on.

Epilogue

It has been almost five years since my father died. I originally started to write this book for my kids. I wanted them to understand the lessons of their grandfather. My hope is that his wisdom, his life, by example, will resonate beyond our family and the Trek family, that others might be as inspired by The Big Guy as those who knew him were. My dad was a one-to-ten guy, and he was also a list guy. For Richie and Courtney, here are my top ten lessons from The Big Guy:

1. To Whom Much Is Given Much Is Required. My dad was a great believer in this saying. He did not grow up with a lot of money, but he ended up accumulating quite a bit along the way. The Big Guy never forgot where he came from and he never forgot that without the help of a lot of people along the way he never would have found the success he enjoyed. He placed a high priority on giving back. In big ways, like giving away large amounts of money to build worthwhile projects like a building for Milwaukee youth arts or urban ecology. In creative ways, like the Burke Scholars. In small ways, like spending countless hours on

121

projects, overlooking every detail to make sure things were done right. He taught all of us that we have a responsibility to our communities and an obligation to share what we have. Everybody has something to contribute, and the act of giving comes with enormous rewards.

2. Follow Your Dreams. My father was for sure a dreamer. He took a big risk at a young age when he bought a majority interest in Roth Distributing with Red. He took a big risk when he started Trek. He took another big risk in staying with Trek when it didn't make money for the first twelve years. Everyone wanted to shut it down, but he kept it going because he had a dream that Trek could be the best bicycle company in the world. Many people only have the ability to look one step down the checkers board. He had the ability to look three or four moves down the board. He followed his dreams, and if he thought he was right, he never gave up. If you decide to devote your life to a business, have a dream and follow it with all that you have. If your dream is to be a teacher, be the *best* teacher. If your dream is to travel the world, do it! Don't let people talk you out of it. Have a dream and pursue it.

3. Be Humble and Put Other People First. For all he accomplished in his seventy-three years, he was a very humble person. The Big Guy never spent much time talking about himself or his accomplishments. He always focused on the other person. Spend your time putting everyone else first and you will go a long way.

Someone once said that it is a good idea to treat regular people like celebrities and celebrities like regular people. He did this very well. Whenever he was talking to someone he made that person feel like they were the most important person in the world.

4. Take Care of Your Body. My dad spent the first forty years of his life being thirty pounds overweight and smoking. When Frank Shorter won the Olympic marathon, The Big Guy took up running. Over the years he ran many marathons, loved to hike, bike, and play tennis. He gave up smoking the pipe and ate well. He was the picture of health at seventy-three. Make sure that you stay active and that you take care of your body. I will never forget being at Trek World in Madison one day when a number of people in their midseventies walked by and they did not look too good. A few minutes later The Big Guy arrived. He looked awesome. He looked good not because he ran that morning; he looked good because for the last thirty-five years he had put a high priority on exercise and eating right.

5. If You Are Going to Do It, Do It Right. When I was a kid, The Big Guy and I would shovel the walk around the house after a snow. This was not my favorite chore and he would always inspect my work. Every time, he finished the inspection with "If you are going to do it, do it right." This was one of the key quotes of his life. No matter what The Big Guy did, he demanded excellence. At Trek, he always wanted to be the best. Let's do it right. New products, marketing cam-

paigns, new buildings, etc. Whatever the project was, he demanded that if we were going to spend time on this, let's do it right. As you go on in life, whether it be something big like starting a new business, or something small like picking out the carpeting for an office, do it right, don't just go through the motions.

6. Do Great Things. The Big Guy was not into small ball. He liked to make a difference. If you are going to start a bike company, let's take Schwinn on. If you are going to build a nonprofit to educate urban kids on the environment, let's do something great, something that will make a difference. Both of you have a great amount of talent and energy; as you move forward in life do something *great*. That might be starting a business, it might be building a family. Whatever it is, do something great. One of my favorite stories is about President Lincoln during the Civil War. On Wednesday nights, he would go down to the Presbyterian Church on K Street and listen to Dr. Gurley give his sermon. Dr. Gurley, knowing that the president might be in attendance, would leave his office, which was right next to the lectern and out of sight, open so that the president could arrive without being seen, listen to the sermon, and depart. On this Wednesday evening the president was joined by his aide. After the sermon they began the walk back to the White House. The aide asked the president, "Mr. President, what did you think of the sermon?" The president responded, "I thought the preparation was

excellent, the material was excellent, and the delivery was excellent." The aide responded, "Well, do you think it was an excellent sermon?" The president responded, "No. It failed because he did not ask us to do anything great." My dad believed in doing great things. At his seventieth birthday party he predicted that he would do one last great thing. As you move forward in life don't spend all of your time on the details of life. Always be thinking of doing something great, and then do it.

7. Think Long Term. I think this was one of his greatest traits. People would always ask him if he would take Trek public. Always the same answer: "No. I don't need the money and I don't need the headaches." Whenever we ran into trouble he always figured out the long-term vision first and then worked back. He loved great causes like Burke Scholars or urban ecology not because of what they were doing today, but because of the benefits to the community twenty years down the road.

8. Be an Optimist. There are two ways to go through life. Being an optimist or being a pessimist. Take your pick. Make a choice. Guess who the most successful people are? My dad was an optimist; the more dire the situation, the more optimistic The Big Guy was. In 1985 when Trek was on the ropes, The Big Guy took control and at Trek's darkest moment he was full of confidence. In 1997 when Trek was having tough times, the person most confident and optimistic about the future was The Big Guy. When he and

I ran our first Boston Marathon, I was in trouble and it was The Big Guy who said don't worry, we will get you to the finish. The Big Guy taught us that life is an amazing game and that we are so lucky to be playing it. Make use of the days that you have, and always understand there will be "bumps in the road." When you hit those bumps have confidence in yourself and always be an optimist. As The Big Guy would tell me, "It beats the hell out of the alternative." Or he would tell me on a bad day at Trek, "You know this situation really isn't so bad, we could be selling refrigerators."

9. Always Have a Goal. Always make sure that you have a set of goals in front of you. My dad loved goals. He loved the story of the guy in the orange shorts, and I have heard him tell that story a hundred times. When Trek sold 6,000 bikes in 1978 I remember him telling me as we were driving out to Trek one day that someday Trek would sell 100,000 bikes. I thought he was nuts . . . One of my great memories was in 1988 when I had the 100,000th bike that we sold taken off the truck and delivered to his office. It was a white Trek 7000 mountain bike and was kept by Trek. At a company meeting in the early 1990s with Trek sales hitting $250 million he gave a speech about the future and he predicted that Trek would hit $1 billion in sales. He had goals for his businesses, he had goals for running a sub-3:30 marathon, and he had goals for the Burke Scholars, and he put together a list once a year with his goals written down. Going through his papers after his death, I saw his goals for

2002 and one of them was "spend more money." It is the only goal that I know he never accomplished. I've learned from The Big Guy, and every year on New Year's I take a piece of paper and write down my top goals for the coming year and I review the list of goals for my life. Take this one piece of advice: Have a set of goals, review them once a year, and keep them in front of you. Do this and you will go far.

10. Learning Never Ends. One of the great lessons of your grandfather's life was that he led a life of learning. The author David McCullough once said that great leaders are great readers and you are what you read. The Big Guy loved to learn and he was an avid reader. He loved *The New York Times,* he read *The Economist, Foreign Affairs,* always had a book going. With The Big Guy learning went beyond books. At forty-five he was a very successful business person but he thought he could learn more so he went back to school and did a one-year program at MIT. He never would have achieved the success that he did if he never went back to MIT. He was always learning. David McCullough is right, you are what you read. If you read about great people, chances are you will become a great person. If you read about great companies your chances of excelling in business go way up. The Big Guy's lesson: never stop learning.

One of my favorite quotes is "A successful life is living up to your potential and giving back to others." If you follow the ten lessons from The Big Guy chances are you will live a very successful life. As I have written this book, I have spent many hours reflecting on my father's life and his impact on me. The Big Guy was a legend and much of who I am is a result of the life lessons he taught me during his life and in his final eighty-eight days. The Big Guy continues to inspire me and I hope that the story of his life and his death will keep his legacy alive and will help to inspire you. The spirit lives on.

JB

Acknowledgments

I have had some great helpers along the way to making this book a reality. I want to thank my mother, Lainey, for all of her help. Lainey read the manuscript a number of times, and most importantly, provided some great insights into The Big Guy's early days. Thank you also to my sisters, Kathy, Mary, Sharon, and Michele. This book would not be what it is without their input. While the focus of this book is my father, so much of his life revolved around our family.

My wife, Tania, played a big role. She provided constant feedback on the content of the book and let me know how special The Big Guy's story was.

I want to thank Dan Bartlett of Public Strategies in Austin. A good friend, Dan took the time to read the book and let me know that it was really good. And Dan put me in touch with Bob Barnett. A special thanks to Bob, who made this book a reality and had the guts on a number of occasions to tell me exactly what he thought. Many thanks to Leah Miller, Dominick Anfuso, and the group at Free Press. Leah gave some great advice and direction, and the book went from good to great.

A special note of thanks to my assistant, Cindy Wagner. A few years ago I gave Cindy an additional title: C.E.O.

Chief Empathy Officer. Cindy is not only my assistant, she is my key advisor on so many different issues, including anything that deals with feelings. I consulted with Cindy on many facets of the book. Because she knew The Big Guy so well, she gave great feedback.

Many thanks to Nicole Sandler for putting in a lot of hours editing the early drafts of the book. Nicole was always available. This book became a labor of love for her, and it shows.

I also want to thank my daughter, Courtney, who spent a lot of time with the manuscript and gave me some great input that really helped the final draft.

Lastly, special thanks to the Trek "family" of employees and retailers. Many of the great moments of my father's life had some connection with Trek. Trek is a family business. It is owned by the Burke family and the Employee Stock Ownership Program, but my father extended that family to include employees and retailers. In one of his final speeches, my father said: "Without all of your support, none of my success would have been possible. While I hope to be around for many more years, I just want to take this opportunity to say, 'Thank you, it has been a great ride.'" My father's incredible story would not have happened without the Trek family, including its employees and retailers.

PHOTO PERMISSIONS AND CREDITS

Endpapers: Courtesy of Trek Bicycle
Prologue: Courtesy of Trek Bicycle
Chapter 1: Family photograph
Chapter 2: Family photograph
Chapter 6: Family photograph
Chapter 12: Courtesy of Trek Bicycle
Memory 4: Family photograph
Memory 7: Family photograph
Memory 9: Family photograph
Memory 11: Jim Moy and the Greater Milwaukee Foundation
Memory 12: Courtesy of Trek Bicycle
Memory 17: Courtesy of Trek Bicycle
Memory 18: Family photograph
Memory 19: Photo by Bruce Lagerquist
Memory 20: Photo by Zach Jones
Chapter 13: Courtesy of Trek Bicycle
Chapter 14: Photo by Mary Johnson
Chapter 15: Photo by Zach Jones

ABOUT THE AUTHOR

John Burke began working at Trek Bicycle in 1984 and has been the company's president since 1997. In addition to leading Trek, John is a founding member of the Bikes Belong Coalition and served as chairman of George W. Bush's President's Council on Physical Fitness and Sports. A native of Wisconsin, John is an avid cyclist and runner and has finished Ironman Wisconsin twice as well as the Boston and New York Marathons. John and his wife, Tania, live in Madison, Wisconsin.